REAL-LIFE
SCIENCE MYSTERIES

Grades 5–8

REAL-LIFE
SCIENCE MYSTERIES

Colleen Kessler

PRUFROCK PRESS INC.
WACO, TEXAS

Prufrock Press Inc.
P.O. Box 8813
Waco, TX 76714-8813
Phone: (800) 998-2208
Fax: (800) 240-0333
http://www.prufrock.com

To the scientists of the future—dream big and you'll lead our country to new discoveries. Never stop questioning.

To Brian—for always seeing my potential, even when I don't.

And to my own future scientists, Trevor, Molly, and Logan—thank you for helping me to see the wonder in every day, whether it is splashing in puddles, hunting for salamanders on a rainy spring night, or making rainbows. Together, we've found science everywhere. I can't wait to see how you each contribute to the world!

Table of Contents

Acknowledgements

Thank you to each person who agreed to be profiled in this book. As I got to know each of you through e-mails, questionnaires, or phone calls, I became more and more excited to be writing this. Each of you contributes to our world in unique and exciting ways. I am honored to have been able to bring your work to kids and teachers everywhere. You are all inspirational.

Thank you to Lacy Compton, editor at Prufrock Press, for giving me the opportunity to work on this really cool project. Not only was it fun, it taught me to look more closely at everyone around me. I found science everywhere, and met—virtually and in real-life—some amazing people.

Thank you, Kelly Dilworth, editor at Prufrock Press, for taking my manuscript and making it shine. Your editorial expertise has made this a book to be proud of.

Finally, thank you to all of my family, friends, and acquaintances— for putting up with my crazy schedule and my requests for contacts, for coming through with those contacts, and for making do with frozen meals or take-out. I couldn't have written this book without your support.

About This Book

You picked up this book, so there is a good chance that you are looking for a more engaging and interesting way to get your students fired up about the science you need to teach them. As a teacher, you need to answer the questions your students often—and rightfully—ask, "Why do I need to learn this?" Or, "When will I ever need this again?" *Real-Life Science Mysteries* was written to help you make your science classes more fun *and* to answer your students' questions of, "What's the point?"

This book provides you with an opportunity to break down the walls of the classroom and invite the real world inside: a world where people—everyday people—are doing science as a career. All over the world, in large cities, small towns, suburbs, and on farms, people face real mysteries and solve them with real science. Some solutions may help create a new species of tulip, while others may save a life, but all are approached with a scientific eye and a willingness to try.

Most kids are curious, but not all continue to look at the world with curiosity and wonder as they grow. This book can help you show your students that there *are* people—adults—out there playing with puzzles, solving mysteries, and indulging in a child-like wonder about the world and how it works. Some of these people have agreed to let you and your students into their minds. They have agreed to give your students a chance to solve some of the mysteries that they have pondered. In this book, you will meet 18 diverse people from across the country working at some of the coolest jobs on the planet.

Each person will share highlights about his or her job, talk about some of the science involved, and challenge your students to solve some problems, observe their world, or experiment with nature.

A common theme in the responses I received from the people profiled in this book was that the science they liked best in school was the science they got to *do*. I tried to include as many hands-on activities as possible to help you insert more *doing* into your science classes and your life. No matter what type of classroom you have or what type of school you are a part of, you will have lots of fun discovering science with your students through the activities in this book.

Each of the men and women interviewed for this book use science in different ways. They may focus primarily on the workings of the human body, why snakes and insects do what they do, how to showcase human structures using the beauty of horticulture, or how to find water deep under the rocks and sand of the desert, but they all have similarities, too. Make sure that you share the connections between domains that the people in each profile share. For example, while Dr. Robert Mason spends time in the fields of Manitoba, Canada, observing wild garter snakes, he documents those observations, investigates the chemistry of the snakes' communication, shares his findings with others, and designs his own inquiries. In fact, the skills of inquiry, observation, and communication are central to everyone's work. These skills are central to science, and to life.

Standards

This book was created with the National Science Education Standards for grades 5–8 in mind, the first of which expects students to develop the abilities necessary to do and understand scientific inquiry (National Research Council, 1996). Each section of this book is tied to inquiry—learning by doing. Students who are actively engaged in their learning retain what they have learned. They internalize it and get excited about it. When you use inquiry and real life as a motivation for and method of learning, kids will want to do it. They will know they can, and perhaps they will want to continue doing science as a career of their own.

I have listed the National Science Education Standards underneath each section title in the Table of Contents. Although there are seven standards, I chose to focus on four: NS.5–8.2 (Physical Science), NS.5–8.3 (Life Science), NS.5–8.4 (Earth and Space Science), and NS.5–8.5 (Science and Technology). I also have chosen to include the process skills covered or discussed in each section. The reason for this method of organization is simple: Standards NS.5–8.1 (Science as Inquiry), NS.5–8.6 (Personal and Social Perspectives), and NS.5–8.7 (History and Nature of Science) are woven throughout each section. These standards integrate naturally into the others and are present in most sections in some form.

Perhaps more important than teaching students about specific science content is teaching them to use science process skills. These skills—observation, communication, classification, measurement, inference, and prediction—are skills that kids will use in every area of their lives. Science is about asking questions and finding answers to those questions. If you want your students to grow up to be discriminating adults, they need to know that they can, and should, question their surroundings and that they have the ability to find out the answers to whatever questions they have.

How to Use This Book

Real-Life Science Mysteries can be used in many ways. For example, it can be treated as a supplement to your science curriculum. Have small groups of students work on a section together, or try the activities as a class. You could even have some high-ability students work on sections individually. You could go section by section, learning about the different jobs one at a time in the order that they are presented, using the experiments and activities as a fun "break" from the everyday curriculum you need to teach. Or, you could look at the skills and standards listed in the Table of Contents and pick the section that relates to the current topic you are presenting. No matter what you choose, you can't go wrong. However you decide to use this book, photocopy the "Hey Kids!" letter on page xv and pass that out first. There is no greater motivation for students than to realize that what they are learning is part of a bigger picture. Science really is something that can help them in their lives—even if they don't want to work in a lab. There are plenty of opportunities out there that allow kids to hang on to their curiosity and make a living they will love.

Most of the activities, investigations, and experiments in this book use everyday materials—those that you would expect to find in a well-equipped middle school science department. I thought about things I could have done with the kids in my own classroom. Sometimes, though, a person suggested an activity that could be done with kids to illustrate a point in his or her interview, show kids what kinds of things he or she does on a daily basis, or show them something that was just plain cool. For these activities, check out the Resources list at the end of the book for websites, books, and science supply outlets.

A few activities, such as "Let's Bake!," may lend themselves better to take-home projects. You may want to offer these as extensions that kids can do at home with adult support. Others, like the sugar glass activity, may be better done as a teacher demonstration. As with anything you plan to do with your students, give careful thought to how it would work in your classroom with your students. For example, if you don't have access to specific computer programs mentioned, like Excel, substitute another data-processing software, or have your students gather data and calculate results by hand. Adapt any of the activities as experiments, demonstrations, extensions, or independent work as you see fit. Enjoy the science . . . and make this book your own.

For materials like tent caterpillars, pond water, soil samples, and bark, you will need to take a walk outside. I am confident that with a little effort, each of these things can be found in nature almost anywhere in the United States. Although species may vary and depend on the season, you *can* find what you need in the great outdoors. I did.

Maybe if you immerse yourself in the beauty and wonder of nature in your hunt for real science to investigate, you will inspire others to do the same. You might become the biology teacher who motivates a future scientist to build off of Dr. Laura Dyer's work as she searches for a cure for heart defects in infants. You may be the chemistry teacher who spurs a would-be chemist to investigate pheromones in insects like Dr. James T. Costa. You might be the person who mentors a future middle school science teacher like Ben Singer. You never know where science will lead you . . .

Our country faces a crisis—the future of science in America is uncertain. Fewer students are seeking advanced degrees in the sciences. We lag behind other countries in the areas of math and science. You can help. You can be the motivator of a future generation of scientists. Your students can be encouraged to be future scientists. One person is all it takes. Will it be you?

Hey Kids

Contrary to what many of you may think, a scientist is *not* a funny-looking person in a white lab coat with glasses and messy hair. A scientist does not spend all of his or her time locked in a lab, sequestered away from other people. A scientist does not do things that the rest of us mere mortals cannot appreciate or understand ...

In fact, scientists are cool! They scale mountains looking for obscure plant and animal life. They create new species of plants by joining two current species together. They go for walks in the woods and draw the salamanders swimming in vernal pools by the light of a rainy moon. They look at virus cells that have been magnified so many times that they look surreal. Most importantly, they follow their passions.

In this book, you will be introduced to many real people working in real science careers. This collection of careers is not complete; it is a sampling of the amazing and exciting world of science. A world where people don't have to completely grow up—ever. It is a world that allows people to play in the mud, look at strange things under the microscope, or build buildings every day of their lives. Not only is science cool—it is so much fun!

Once you've examined the careers included in this book, look around you. Try to figure out just what science is being done by the person who controls the landfill where your trash is taken on garbage day. Is the butcher at the supermarket using science as he prepares your meat? How about the chef at the restaurant downtown? Does she use science to create fantastic new recipes?

Be curious about your world. Let me know what you discover as you develop your passions and find mentors to teach you about their interests. I look forward to hearing from you—the future of science!

—Colleen

http://www.colleen-kessler.com

Name: _____ Date: _____

Director of Education
Mark Baldwin, New York

The name Roger Tory Peterson is synonymous with nature and field guides. The Roger Tory Peterson Institute in Jamestown, NY, honors Peterson's work and continues his legacy by promoting the study of nature.

Mark Baldwin, Director of Education for the Roger Tory Peterson Institute, has a cool job. He is a writer, professor, trainer, and coach. He devotes his time to helping others develop an awareness and appreciation for nature. Mostly working with adults, he conducts professional development for teachers to help them become better at what they do. He says, "The point of all this professional development is to help teachers to be curious and excited about the world around them—just like scientists themselves, and to understand better what science is all about."

To be successful at a job like Mark's, you need to "love nature and be endlessly curious about it. You also need to love science, the special way we come to learn more about nature. You need to love people, because you're always learning from them. And you need to love reading, writing, speaking, and listening—communicating—because you find yourself doing that all the time." Communication seems to be a common theme in science jobs.

Speak Up!

Communication is important in life—and it is particularly important to those working in the sciences. Although people like Mark enjoy what they do on a daily basis, and would probably be happy to go on observing nature or making scientific discoveries on their own, they need to share their knowledge with the public. Only by increasing public awareness and fostering a love of science and nature in other people will their careers really have a positive impact. In this activity, you will present to a group of people in order to build their awareness of a science topic that interests you.

Materials

- Research materials
- A group of people willing to hear your presentation
- Any materials that you need to create visual aids

Procedure

1. Choose a topic that you are interested in learning more about.
   - You might want to learn about an organism, a topic such as the weather, or an issue like the conservation of water or the protection of coral reefs.

2. Use the Internet, books, magazines, and other resources to learn as much as you can about your topic.
   - Enlist the help of local experts. Call a nearby university and see if a biology professor can tell you about his or her interests. Go on a walk through the woods with a naturalist.

3. Prepare a presentation about your topic.
   - Make any notes you need in order to present effectively. (Some people like to write out the things that they will say, while others like to prepare a list of key points that they will cover.)
   - You may want to include photographs, a poster, or a diagram.

4. Share your learning or your position with your class, your family, or another group of interested people.

In middle school, Mark was very interested in science. Unfortunately, he hated most of his classes. In fact, in eighth grade, he decided that he might want to become a science teacher because his science teacher was doing such an awful job! He felt that he could do better than have kids read out of a textbook and answer other people's questions. After all, science is all about discovering, then answering, your own questions. To do this, you must become a good observer.

Mark notes, "All science investigations start by making an observation, but, oddly enough, most science teachers don't know how to teach this. I teach them how to see more accurately themselves and how to teach others as well."

In order to teach this well, Mark must constantly hone his own observation skills. "I try to keep a field journal on a regular basis that contains my notes and sketches about what I observe in the world around me, along with notes about what I have learned from my observations."

Keeping a Field Journal

Journaling about what you see in the field—in nature—is a good way to record and enhance your observational skills. When you combine drawing and writing, you use more of your senses to process what you observe and therefore remember and appreciate more of the nature around you. In this activity, you will record what you feel, see, hear, and touch, involving as many of your senses as possible.

Materials

- Nature journal (e.g., notebook, three-ring binder with blank pages, sketchbook)
- Pencils
- Watercolor pencils
- Watercolor brush
- Bark, leaves, sticks, or other materials found in nature

Procedure

1. Pick up a piece of bark, a leaf, a stick, or something else from outside.
2. Sit down and close your eyes, still holding your object.
3. Feel the object. Note the texture, size, and any features that make the object unique.
4. Now, put the object behind your back and open your eyes. Using your nature journal, draw what you felt when you held the object in your hand. Focus on those unique textures that you felt. Draw from your sense of touch.
5. Pick the object back up and add details to your drawing. Add color using your watercolor pencils.
6. Record the date, time, and location in your journal.
7. You also may want to jot down any thoughts or other observations about the object in a few sentences beneath your drawing.
8. Do activities like this often. Get outside and train yourself to observe nature keenly. Compare objects that are similar to the one that you recorded today in different weather conditions and seasons.

A big part of Mark's job is to enjoy the outdoors in the company of people who are super excited about nature. "That combination of being outside with people who share a love of learning about birds, insects, plants, and other living things, means my work is never boring. That's cool."

"That combination of being outside with people who share a love of learning about birds, insects, plants, and other living things, means my work is never boring. That's cool."

Education Program Specialist
Shannon Trimboli, Kentucky

"Science is fun! It can take place anywhere and anyone can be a scientist," says Shannon Trimboli, Education Program Specialist for the Mammoth Cave International Center for Science and Learning in Kentucky. And Shannon would know. She spends her days helping scientists do research at the national park and then teaching others about that research. Right now, Shannon is working with a group of middle schoolers to study temperature fluctuations in cave rivers compared to surface rivers.

> "Science is fun! It can take place anywhere and anyone can be a scientist"

Along with the research director, Shannon and the middle school students are conducting important scientific research at the park. They have discovered that, although most springs carry cave water out to surface water, when the Green River reaches a certain level, one of the springs starts flowing backwards. It takes surface water into the cave! This strange phenomenon has been known for years, but nothing has been done to study it before now. Using data loggers to measure the temperature of the water at several spots in the cave and then on the surface, students are trying to determine how often, and for how long, this spring flows backwards.

This research—conducted by kids like you—is important. There are many scientists who are interested in the project and want to know what the students find out.

The research that these middle school students are doing was featured in their local newspaper, sharing with everyone the message that kids <u>can</u> do something scientifically meaningful. Check it out at: http://www.thenewsenterprise.com/cgi-bin/c2.cgi?053+article+News.Local+201002191811310530530O2.

What Is the Best Insulator?

Because it wouldn't be practical, or even possible, for everyone reading this book to head out into nearby caves and test water temperature fluctuation between surface water and cave water, we'll test water temperature in a different way. Most materials—from packed leaves to crumpled up pieces of paper—have some ability to slow heat flow. This is called insulation. How much does the material of an insulator affect the constancy of water temperature? Find out in this activity.

Materials

- Several different materials to use as insulators:
    - Crumpled paper
    - Cloth scraps
    - Leaves
    - Sand or dirt
    - Sticks or wood scraps
    - Unbreakable thermometer, one for each insulator

- Plastic cups with lids, one for each insulator
- Lidded box slightly larger than the cups, one for each insulator
- Clock/timer
- Paper or journal for recording data
- Pencil

Procedure

1. Make a hole in each box and cup lid just big enough for your thermometer to slide in and out easily.
2. Put a layer of each type of insulation in the bottom of each box.
3. Place a cup in the center of each box, on top of the insulation layer.
4. Pack insulation material tightly around the cup so that the box is filled.
5. Fill each cup with warm water.
6. Place the lid tightly on each cup.
7. Pack more insulation on top of each cup, being careful not to cover the thermometer hole.

8. Put the lid on the box and lower a thermometer through the hole in each box, through the hole in each cup, and into the water.
9. After 2–3 minutes, pull the thermometer out. Record the time and the temperature for each cup of water.
10. Put the thermometers back in each cup.
11. Continue checking the temperature of each cup of water every 15 minutes until the temperature stops changing. It has reached room temperature. (*Note.* Each cup may reach room temperature at a different time. Continue recording temperatures for each cup until all have reached room temperature.)
12. Answer the following questions:
    - Which cup took the longest to reach room temperature?
    - What material insulated that cup?
    - Why do you think that material insulated the water so well?
    - Which cup reached room temperature the quickest?
    - What material insulated that cup?
    - Why do you think that material was a poor insulator?

When Shannon was young, she loved learning about plants and animals. Like many students, her favorite part of science class came when she was actually *doing* something. "Outside activities were always my favorite," she says, "but I also enjoyed looking at slides under the microscope, especially if those slides contained drops of pond water." She enjoyed playing outside, looking at different plants, trying to get close to native animals like deer without spooking them, and watching birds fly overhead.

To be good at Shannon's job, someone would need to be curious, love to learn new things, and enjoy all different types of science. Even though her main love is biology, Shannon needs to know about geology, hydrology, archaeology, and other types of science. "You also need to be interested in going out into woods, caves, streams, fields, and be willing to get hot and dirty when you are conducting research." In addition, it is important to be willing to share your work with others. An important part of Shannon's job is working with people to teach them about new findings. As a result, she needs to be interested in photography, writing, and speaking.

"Find something you love, and never give up on that dream."

Studying Pond Water

Pond water is a cool thing to study. Every drop has the potential to contain lots of different organisms. In this study, you will collect pond water samples to observe the organisms present and discover if they vary by location. Ideally, a teacher, several adults, or several students can collect three or four pond water samples from different locations. If it is not possible to collect water from different locations, an adult may collect water from different depths, at different times of the day, or you may stretch this activity through different seasons and collect one sample per season to compare results.

Note to teacher or other adult. If there is a pond on your school grounds or nearby, consider taking your students to collect samples themselves. Discuss water safety and the importance of collecting samples at the edge of the water so as not to fall in. Having students collect their own water samples adds to the authenticity of the activity and gives them ownership of the experiment.

Materials

- Thermometers
- 1-liter bottle per location for water collection
- Pond water, preferably from different locations
- Hand lens
- Microscope
- Concave microscope slides
- Pipette
- Baby food jars or Petri dishes

Procedure

1. Collect pond water samples.
2. Take the temperature of the water at each location.
3. Write the location, time collected, and temperature on the 1-liter container that each sample will be collected in.
4. Dip your container into the water, collecting any algae or other nearby plant material. Pull the container through the water quickly so that the organisms do not escape. Do this at each location.
5. Once you are back in the classroom, observe your samples.
6. Identify and record the type and number of any visible organisms using a hand lens. (To make identification easier, use a pipette to pull individual organisms and a bit of water into a Petri dish or baby food jar placed on white paper.)

7. Once all visible organisms have been identified, transfer smaller organisms or water drops to concave slides and observe the slides under a microscope.
8. Repeat the steps above for each location.
9. Make a chart or graph showing the number of different organisms that you found at each location.
10. Compare the charts.

Shannon shares an important piece of advice with young people: "Find something you love, and never give up on that dream." When she was in college, she wanted to conduct research, teach other people about what she was learning, and get nonscientists involved in research. At the time, there weren't many ways to do that. Now there are. Citizen science is one of those ways.

Citizen science is a term used to describe projects that everyday volunteers can get involved in. People work side by side with scientists or in their own backyards to conduct research. Their research is then shared with scientists and analyzed along with research from other people participating in the project. It is a wonderful way for both scientists and volunteers to work together. Scientists can get access to data from a wide range of locations and subjects, and everyday people can feel as if they are making a difference in the world of science.

Some Web Sources for Citizen Science Projects

Cornell Lab of Ornithology
http://www.birds.cornell.edu/netcommunity/citsci/projects

New Jersey Audubon Society
http://www.njaudubon.org/SectionCitizenScience/
WhatisCitizenScience.aspx

EarthTrek
http://www.goearthtrek.com

National Wildlife Federation
http://www.nwf.org

Science Teacher
Ben Singer, Ohio

Ben Singer is an eighth-grade science teacher in Beachwood, OH. He teaches subjects such as scientific inquiry, forces and motion, energy, astronomy, Earth science, and chemistry.

Teachers are responsible for creating and presenting lessons that align with the standards set forth by the state department of education and then measuring a student's understanding of the material. Ben says, "I have always found the explanation for the why and how of things to be interesting, but I don't think I started developing a serious interest in science until high school."

"Discovery and experimentation define the essence of science."

According to Ben, "Discovery and experimentation define the essence of science." Therefore, he teaches a discovery-based curriculum. Lessons are created so that students are actively responsible for discovering their own answers through activities and experimentation.

"In addition to teaching students science based on discovery and experimentation, we use technology every day. Every student in our middle school has a laptop so we can use Excel to collect, organize, and graph data. We use the Internet to conduct scientific research or to access online simulations of scientific concepts. I try to design lessons so that students are doing 'real-world' science and using technology on a daily basis."

How Much Water Do You Use?

Collecting real data is a great way to see how science applies to your own life. Conservation is important in today's ecological climate. In this activity, you will use an Excel spreadsheet to collect and analyze data about the water you use in a day. Is it a lot? A little? How good are you at conserving water?

Materials

- Computer with Excel
- Internet access
- Notebook and pencil

Procedure

1. On a piece of paper in your notebook, write the following categories:
   - Baths
   - Showers
   - Teeth brushing
   - Hand and face washing
   - Shaving
   - Dishwasher
   - Dish washing by hand
   - Laundry
   - Toilet flushes
   - Glasses of water

2. For one day, keep your notebook and pencil with you from the time you wake up until you go to bed.
3. Record each time you do one of the things on your list.
4. Go to the U.S. Geological Survey website (http://ga.water.usgs.gov/edu/sq3.html) and use the water science questionnaire to calculate how much water you used.
5. Record the amount in each category in your notebook.
6. Create an Excel spreadsheet and enter your data.
7. Using Excel, graph your total water usage, what percentage each category uses, and determine if and where you can cut back.
8. Share your results with your family and challenge them to keep track of their own water usage for a day.

9. If they take you up on that challenge, collect their data using Excel and create a graph displaying your family's total water usage.

10. Have a meeting to discuss where your family uses the most water. Make a plan for cutting back.

Ben usually starts his day around 7 a.m. so that he has time to prepare before students arrive at 7:50. Each day, he teaches six science classes—four general and two advanced—and has a teaming period where he meets with other eighth-grade teachers to discuss issues within the grade. He has one planning period each day to work on administrative tasks like grading papers and planning lessons.

One of the coolest things about Ben's job is "seeing students get excited about science." Ben notes, "One example would be science fair, which is one of the major projects we do each year. The students work on a scientific question, design an experiment to test their theory, gather information, and analyze that information. Then, they have to present that information at a science fair to science professionals from the community who come in to talk to them about their work. It is exciting to see the students talk to science professionals and to hear the positive feedback that these community members give about our students."

"I think science is very interesting, so if I can enhance or develop that interest in my students, that is rewarding to me. One of the difficult things about teaching is that you never really know the impact you are making. You teach with enthusiasm and a love for the subject, and hope that in some way you make an impression on your students."

He adds, "In my opinion, teaching is one of the greatest jobs there is. You have the opportunity to mold your students and their future on a daily basis. As a teacher, you will never discover cures for diseases or journey to Mars, but your students might."

"As a teacher, you will never discover cures for diseases or journey to Mars, but your students might."

Developing a Science Fair Project

- Your **research question** is the most important part of the scientific method. What are you trying to find out? Your project will be designed to answer that question. Sometimes, a research question can be formed as a statement, in which case it is called the **problem** or **problem statement**.
- Your **hypothesis** is an educated guess and is written as a statement. This is what you believe will be the outcome of your experiment.
- Design an **experiment** to test your hypothesis.
- Your experiment will contain elements that do not change. These are called **controlled** or **dependent variables**. It also will contain elements that change, called **manipulated** or **independent variables**.
- Your **control** is a sample that has all of the elements of other samples, but it is not exposed to manipulated variables.
- You need to **observe** your experiment carefully. What do you see, smell, hear, and so forth? Use all of your senses.
- While observing your experiment, **collect data** by recording the progress. You may be recording observations, temperatures, pH, color, growth, or other values.
- Scientists keep a **record** of their observations and data. You can journal about your observations and data, too.
- **Data** are the values that you write down as your experiment progresses.
- It is important to illustrate your data so that others can interpret them easily. To do this, you may want to create **charts** or **graphs**.
- List all of the **materials** that you will need.
- Your **procedure** should be written as a detailed, step-by-step description of how you conducted your experiment. It should be so detailed that anyone who wants to can replicate your experiment exactly.
- Your **results** should be written in a statement that explains and interprets the data you collected.
- Write a detailed **conclusion** that summarizes your research and results. You should answer your research question and make a statement that tells whether or not your data supported your hypothesis. Try to include reasons why you think your hypothesis was or was not supported.
- You may want to include an **application** statement. This explains how the knowledge gained by your experiment can be used.

- You should recognize the people, websites, books, and other sources that helped you complete your experiment. These are called your **resources** and are very important to the success of your project.
- All of these components should be gathered and displayed according to the specifications of the science fair in which you are participating. If you are designing and conducting an experiment for fun, make sure that you share your results with someone. The best science is the science that you share with others!

© Prufrock Press Inc. • Real-Life Science Mysteries

This page may be photocopied or reproduced with permission for single classroom use only.

19

Naturalist
Heather L. Montgomery, Alabama

When Heather L. Montgomery was in seventh grade, she had a life science teacher who turned her on to nature. She learned to go outside and figure things out. "No one told me the answers to why certain fish lived in a stream and others lived at the bottom of a river. I had to discover it for myself. I've been hooked on nature ever since."

Now, Heather is a naturalist and environmental educator. Most of her time is spent taking groups into the woods to learn about nature. She hikes canyons and catches bugs in a creek. "My family thinks it's funny," she says, "because when I was a little girl, I hated dirt and was scared of spiders. Now, I paint my face with dirt and let spiders crawl up my arm. I discovered that once I learned about something like spiders, it was no longer scary."

"I paint my face with dirt and let spiders crawl up my arm. I discovered that once I learned about something like spiders, it was no longer scary."

Spectacular Spiders

Spiders are fascinating to watch. Whether they are spinning webs or lying in wait for a tasty meal, they are cool creatures. This activity will work best if you have a spider to watch for a few days. You can find one on a window to observe, locate one outside in a sheltered location, or capture one for a pet. The instructions below include the details you need to capture your own spider. If you decide to watch a spider in its natural habitat, skip to the observation steps.

Materials

- Plastic or glass terrarium or large jar with air holes drilled in the lid
- Potting soil
- Sticks, dead leaves, plants (live or artificial), stones
- Small water dish (a yogurt container lid will work)
- Prey (crickets from a pet store or insects from pesticide-free locations outside)

Procedure

1. Prepare your spider's home by layering potting soil on the bottom of your terrarium. Place a water dish in a corner and fill with a small amount of water. Decorate the terrarium with sticks, stones, and plants to provide climbing, hiding, and web-building structures for your spider.
2. Catch your spider by gently coaxing it into a small jar using the lid. Carry your jar to your terrarium and drop your pet inside. (*Note.* You should have an adult with you as you hunt for your pet. Some spider species may bite.)
3. Capture or purchase prey insects to feed your spider once or twice a week.
4. When you are ready to feed your spider (either your pet, or one you are watching in its natural habitat), take one of the prey insects and carefully place it in the spider's web.
5. What does your spider do? Does it eat the insect immediately? Does it wrap it and save it for later? (If your spider is hungry, it may eat right away. It will do this by injecting its prey with enzymes that dissolve the insect's insides. The spiders then drink the liquefied "bug soup." If the spider is not hungry, it will bite its prey to paralyze it, wrap it in silk, and put it aside for later.)

To be good at Heather's job, you need to have a lot of energy. She leads night hikes and puts in long days. When she was in middle school, she was shy and didn't like getting up in front of people. But she has since discovered that a passion for learning, and an excitement about something can help you overcome your fears. "The cool thing is, I learned that when you want to do something, you can overcome all kinds of obstacles. I can now stand up in front of a group of 150 people and share the night sky with them without being nervous at all."

Hiking at night, without a flashlight, is one of Heather's favorite things to do. Studying katydids and their calls, screech owls, or glow worms (larvae of different types of beetles) dotting the creek bank like a sky full of stars, are some of the wonders she gets to enjoy. It is important, though, not to hike at night without an adult or someone who knows the area well.

Learning About Larvae

You may have encountered a mealworm before—in your kitchen! Mealworms are the larva of the darkling beetle and sometimes get into cereal boxes. They are common prey of rodents, reptiles, birds, and other beetles. Therefore, they often can be purchased at a local pet store relatively inexpensively. Get to know a mealworm and learn about its natural behaviors.

Materials

- Mealworm(s)
- Small container (e.g., jar with lid holes, plastic terrarium)
- Oatmeal
- Apple or potato chunk
- Stopwatch
- Flashlight
- Vinegar
- Flat toothpicks
- Cotton swab
- Straw
- Paper towels—one damp, one dry
- Paper

Procedure

1. Make a habitat for your mealworm(s) by filling your container half full of oatmeal. Put your apple or potato chunk on top of the oats. The oats will feed your mealworms and the potato or apple will provide them with water.
2. Observe a mealworm before putting it in its habitat.
3. Gently place the flat end of the toothpick under its legs so that it can grab onto it.
4. Lift the mealworm up. What does it look like? How many legs does it have?
5. Set your mealworm down on the paper.

6. Gently blow some air through the straw at your mealworm's head. What does it do?
7. Use the toothpick to touch its antennae very gently. What does it do?
8. Dip your cotton swab in the vinegar and place it in front of your mealworm. What does it do?
9. Put the mealworm right next to the base of its terrarium. What does it do when it gets close to that edge?
10. Shine your flashlight on the front half of your mealworm. What does it do?
11. Put a damp paper towel next to a dry one. Put your mealworm on the line where they touch. What does it do?
12. Why do you think that your mealworm reacted the way it did each time? How could these reactions protect it from harm in the wild?
13. Place your mealworm on top of the oatmeal in its new home. What does it do? Does it stay on top or does it dig into the oatmeal? Why do you think it does this?
14. Observe your mealworm each day, noting any changes in its life cycle that you can. How long do you think it will take before your mealworm becomes an adult darkling beetle? How long did it actually take? Keep this habitat for as long as you like.

Being a naturalist like Heather is a cool way to use science every day. It also is a great way to help others do science every day. Researchers visit the property where Heather works to study salamanders, and she gets to help students who visit the property walk in the footsteps of those researchers. She leads groups in collecting water samples from clear-running streams and comparing them to a sample from a chocolate-milk colored stream. Although she has degrees in biology and environmental education, Heather studies every day. She says, "There are so many amazing animals and plants to learn about."

Drinking Water Quality

Water breaks apart into hydrogen and hydroxide ions and then comes together again. Many other substances also have hydrogen and hydroxide ions. If something has more hydrogen ions than hydroxide ions, it is called an acid. Acids taste sour. Have you ever tasted lemon juice? It is an acid! Substances with more hydroxide ions are called basic or alkaline. These are bitter. Baking soda is one example of a bitter alkaline. You can measure the pH of water to determine its acidity. When water is pure—the number of hydrogen ions is equal to the number of hydroxide ions—it is called neutral. It has a pH of 7. Water that is too acidic or alkaline may harm us.

Materials

- Several clean glass jars
- Tap water
- Bottled spring water
- Distilled water
- Rainwater (if possible)
- Pond water
- pH test strips (litmus paper)

Procedure

1. Set the water samples in labeled jars out where they can be tested.
2. Dip a fresh pH test strip in each sample.
3. Remove the test strip immediately and hold it level for several seconds.
4. Compare the pH strip to the color chart that came with the strips.
5. Record the pH of each sample.
6. Answer the following questions:
   - Which is closest to neutral?
   - Which samples are safe to drink?
   - Which are not?

Heather's love of science extends through all aspects of her life. She uses this love in her daily work as a naturalist. She also uses it to craft nonfiction books for kids. Check out her book titles at her website: http://www.heatherlmontgomery.com/Publications.html.

Wildlife Officer
Dave Shinko, Ohio

If you enjoy being outdoors and have a desire to protect the lives of animals, you may want to think about becoming a wildlife officer like Dave Shinko. Dave is a supervisor in Ohio. Ohio has 88 counties, each with a wildlife officer assigned to it. A wildlife officer uses science every day.

Wildlife officers determine the populations of the various wildlife species in their area in order to set the hunting, fishing, and trapping seasons and limits. An officer must be able to identify animal species that are native to the state. Wildlife officers set their own schedules, trying to be around when they have a better chance of interacting with the public. "Officers are encouraged to work when there are favorable weather conditions. If it is a cold and rainy Monday morning in late March, we would expect to see fewer participants than if it were a sunny Friday morning in the same month," Dave explains.

A strong interest in wildlife, and getting outside, is important if you want to become a wildlife officer. "I would encourage kids to get the family involved [in their interests] by participating in outdoor pursuits like hunting, fishing, and trapping. When I was young, my father, grandfather, uncle, and I frequently fished Lake Erie and local farm ponds." Learning to observe local wildlife is important, too.

> A strong interest in wildlife, and getting outside, is important if you want to become a wildlife officer.

Blind Yourself

It is important for wildlife officers to be able to identify state wildlife species. An officer must be able to enforce trapping, hunting, and fishing laws. To do that, he must be able to look at a person's catch and determine if he or she is within the law regarding the number of each species caught. Although you can't go out and search a hunter's, angler's, or trapper's bag, you can stake out wildlife in your own backyard or your schoolyard and learn to identify each species.

Materials

- Large cardboard appliance box
- Sticks
- Leaves
- Hot glue
- Craft knife
- Bird, reptile, and mammal field guides for your area
- Journal and pencil (optional)
- Camera (optional)

Procedure

1. Find a spot in your backyard or your schoolyard that is frequently visited by local wildlife (e.g., a pond, a bird feeder, a clutch of trees).
2. Position your box so that it lies on its side with the bottom facing the wildlife area.
3. With the craft knife, cut a slit in the solid bottom of the box (the part pointing toward the wildlife area). This will be your window, so make it small enough that you won't be visible to animals, but large enough that you can still see out of it.
4. Using a hot glue stick, attach leaves to the outside of the box to camouflage your blind. Throw a pillow or a blanket on the floor, and grab your journal (for writing about and sketching what you see), your camera (for photographing what you see), and your field guides. Get comfortable, and hang out for a while.
5. Notice what wildlife comes close to your hideout. Enjoy your close-up view of nature.

In college, Dave earned a bachelor of science degree in wildlife management. He studied ornithology, biology, mammalogy, botany, and zoology. "A significant portion of my time was spent studying an animal's habitat and the animal itself." Throughout the year, wildlife officers must attend training sessions that focus on things like firearm tactics, self-defense, and law reviews.

A wildlife officer is a "jack of all trades."

A wildlife officer is a "jack of all trades," according to Dave. "One day, we are assisting our fish management personnel with electrofishing or walleye netting. The next day, we may be enforcing wildlife regulations or conducting a school program with live raptors."

One of the most important charges a wildlife officer has is to enforce the laws and regulations surrounding hunting, fishing, and

trapping in their state. The officer checks to make sure that hunters and anglers (men and women who fish using a hook) have the proper licenses. He or she also checks to make sure that hunters and anglers have not gone over their bag limits, or that they have not caught more animals than allowed. "Officers are required to investigate alleged criminal activity," Dave notes. "Although most anglers and hunters are law abiding, ethical, and responsible, we are required to arrest and charge those individuals who do not comply with our laws."

Dave's biggest motivation is that, by arresting and convicting wildlife offenders, he is helping to contribute to the overall health of wildlife resources and the agency. "I hope that the presence of wildlife officers across the state will deter individuals from committing wildlife offenses." He reminds us, "The management of Ohio's [and any state's] wildlife is almost entirely supported by those who purchase hunting, fishing, and trapping licenses." Get outside and experience nature! You may decide to become a wildlife officer and dedicate your life to the wildlife in your state.

To find out more about your specific state's wildlife agencies, check out the list of links on the U.S. Fish and Wildlife Service's website: http://www.fws.gov/offices/statelinks.html.

Children's Science Writer
Loree Griffin Burns, Massachusetts

A children's book writer featured in a book about scientists? Absolutely! Even if Loree Griffin Burns *didn't* have a Ph.D. in biochemistry—which she does—her science writing itself is perfect to talk about in a discussion of science careers. To all those kids who like to write stories, but also love science, you can follow both of those passions, and turn them into an exciting career. Loree says, "Science writers are typically curious, skeptical, and organized people with a flair for communicating ideas. A sense of adventure is a huge bonus!"

As a science writer, Loree's days are never quite the same. Most of them find her sitting at her desk and reading or writing. Sometimes, she writes proposals for new books she wants to write; other times, she writes the books themselves. Writers "do a lot of editing and rewriting (and rewriting and rewriting)."

Some of her favorite days involve getting out in the field to research new books. "This work thrills me," she says, "because I get to tag along with scientists as they do their research, usually learning about subjects that are entirely new to me. I've combed beaches on both coasts, collected water samples in the Pacific Ocean, inspected bee hives in full beekeeping gear, and let an apitherapist sting me so we could collect an image for a book on honeybees."

An apitherapist uses honeybee venom to treat a wide variety of conditions and illnesses. To learn more about apitherapy, check out the American Apitherapy Society's website: http://www.apitherapy.org.

Research a Nonfiction Book

Some people say that you should write what you know. Others suggest that you should write what you want to know. Good nonfiction writers do a little of both. They start with a nugget of information that they heard or remember from their past. Then, they research the topic further. And further. And still further, until they have more information than they will need. Think about something that you know a little bit about, may want to learn more about, and could turn into an interesting nonfiction book. Then, hit the Internet and library and talk to local experts. Find out all you can about your topic.

Materials

- Research materials
- Expert mentors

Procedure

1. Decide on a topic, and narrow it down to something specific. For example, if you are interested in coral reefs, then maybe you want to learn about reefs, coral polyps, and threats to the reefs. You may then decide to focus on natural threats to the reef, such as the crown-of-thorns starfish, because there is already a lot out there about human threats to the reef.
2. Pull together resources: books, magazine articles, websites, and expert interviews. Maybe you could e-mail the head marine biology instructor at a university in Florida and ask her for information. If you live near a reef, go snorkeling with an adult. Go to an aquarium to observe the animals of the reef.
3. Take notes in whatever way makes the most sense to you. Some writers like to organize their notes on index cards, organized by topic. Others like to outline. Still others just take continuous notes on paper and go back to organize these notes later.
4. File your notes away to be pulled out in the next activity.

Loree's books highlight stories of science and discovery. She believes her job "is to create books that excite, inspire, and inform readers." Not an easy task! Kids with an interest in writing should hone their skills. They should read widely and all the time, focusing on the types of books and articles they want to write. "Most importantly, write. And write. And write some more."

Write a Book

OK, so you have a lot of research about a topic. Now, how do you pull out the most interesting information and create a book? First, don't worry about getting your draft perfect right off the bat. Writers, as Loree said, write, and write, and write, and write some more. There is no such thing as a perfect first draft. You will need to go through your notes and find the nugget that makes the most interesting story, pull that out, and write.

Materials

- Your research from the last activity
- Writing materials
- Book-binding materials

Procedure

1. Write the first draft of your nonfiction book. The key to remember about your initial draft is that, even though this is nonfiction, it should not be a list of facts. Think about how you can tell the story of your topic in a clear and entertaining way. Pull out the most interesting pieces from your research. Use those. If you need ideas for how to make nonfiction interesting, pick up Loree's books: *Tracking Trash* and *The Hive Detectives*. Go to a library and ask the youth librarian to help you find interesting nonfiction books or articles to read. Pay special attention to how these books are written to tell a story.
2. Once your draft is written, put it aside for a few days. Then, pull it back out and look at it with fresh eyes. What could you do to make it better? Can you add or delete some information?
3. Next, get someone you trust to read through your manuscript and offer suggestions. Remember that no draft is perfect. Get a reader who will be honest with you—a teacher, a parent, or a friend. You don't want a reader who will tell you that your draft is great in order to spare your feelings. You *know* that work needs to be done on it. You want a reader who will tell you what you can do to make the book better.
4. Take the suggestions and decide which you agree with and want to use, and which you want to discard. Revise your manuscript.
5. Now, type a final draft on the computer and print it out.

6. Use your book-binding materials to create a book. Design (or have an artistic friend design) a cover and illustrations for your book.
7. Share your finished product with someone.

The coolest thing about science writing for Loree is the exploring that she gets to do. "I live with a certain topic, honey bees, for example, for a year or two . . . but when my book is finished, I get to choose an entirely new topic to study for awhile. And once I've chosen a topic, I can totally immerse myself in it. It's the perfect job for someone who is curious about lots of different things . . . someone like me!"

Biologist
Robert Mason, Oregon

Dr. Robert Mason is lucky to be doing exactly what he has always wanted to do. "I knew from middle school onward that I wanted to be a biologist. I wanted to work with wild animals, and I wanted to do field work." He gets to do both, as well as teach classes, in his role as the Chair of the Biology Program at Oregon State University.

One of the coolest parts of his job, though, is the research that he conducts each spring when he travels to Manitoba, Canada. "For about six weeks, we study the mating behavior and physiology of the red-sided garter snake. We do field work all day, every day, during that time. When the weather is good, we're out in the field; when it's not so good, we work at the field station."

"I knew from middle school onward that I wanted to be a biologist. I wanted to work with wild animals, and I wanted to do field work."

Friction and Locomotion

Snakes are cool to watch. Whether you are repulsed by them or fascinated by them, it is difficult to tear your eyes away when a snake is moving nearby. Typically, people think of the sidewinding motion some snakes use to move. However, snakes move in other ways too. They move laterally when waves of muscle contractions move down their body, pushing them forward. Some move like an accordion in concertina motion. They pull themselves into folds (like the instrument) and straighten themselves out to move. Rectilinear motion is a straight movement that happens when large snakes use their belly scales to grip the ground and creep forward. Snakes also can climb, jump, and coil up and strike. They can use a corkscrew motion to swim.

However they move, all snakes use friction to move themselves forward. Friction allows their scales to grip the ground and use it to push off. They can move their scales one at a time to get a better grip on uneven surfaces, or they can move them as one using the force of all of their scales at the same time. If you have access to a pet snake, try watching it move across different surfaces—wood floors, tile, carpet, sand, plastic drop cloth, and so forth. See if you can figure out which surface would require the snake to use the most force to propel itself. If you can't watch a real snake, try the following experiment to see which surface creates the most friction, therefore making it easier for a snake to cross.

Materials

- Various surfaces to test (e.g., wood floors, ceramic tile, carpet, sand or sandpaper, plastic)
- Small cardboard box
- Thin rope
- Scissors
- Weights (e.g., books, blocks)
- Spring scale

Procedure

1. Poke a hole in the box with the scissors.
2. Tie the rope around the box.
3. Fill the box with a few books or blocks to weigh it down.
4. Place the box on a wood floor.
5. Hook the spring scale to the end of the rope that is not tied to the box.

6. Pull the box across the floor, noting how much force is exerted by reading the spring scale.
7. Repeat this activity on all of the other surfaces.
8. Answer the following questions:
   - Which surfaces required more force? Why?
   - Would it be easier for a snake to move across a tile floor than carpet? Why?

Robert notes, "I think the coolest part of my job is when we get some results from an experiment and, all of a sudden, we understand why the garter snakes are doing this or that, when just the day before it was still a mystery to us. I love to figure out what makes the garter snakes do what they do."

Middle school science was at its best for Robert when he was learning about how things really happen and why. For example, although he knew that there were different seasons, and each had different conditions, he loved learning that the seasons exist because of the rotation of the Earth around the sun and the tilt of the Earth's axis. He watched nature programs and read as many books about animals as he could: "I liked to try and identify as many species as I could, and I would practice on the birds in my backyard or by identifying all of the snakes, frogs, and turtles in the marshes and swamps around our home."

"I think the coolest part of my job is when we get some results from an experiment and, all of a sudden, we understand why the garter snakes are doing this or that, when just the day before it was still a mystery to us."

Snake Skin

Snakes shed layers of their skin as they grow. As they don't have arms and legs, they must rub up against objects to help get the dead skin off. How difficult do you think this is? Try the activity below to see how good you would be at shedding your skin if you were a snake. Make it more fun by getting a few friends together and having a competition. See who can shed their snakeskin the quickest—and who would make the best snake!

Materials

- Pantyhose (tight-fitting, knee-high)

Procedure

1. Pull the knee-high pantyhose onto your arm as high as it will go. Make sure it fits snugly.
2. Try to get your "skin" off without using your other hand.
3. Like a snake in the wild, you may want to rub up against something to help you.
4. Answer the folowing questions:
   - How difficult was this task?
   - Why might it be easier for other reptiles like lizards to shed their skin?

Robert shares this advice with young people: "Be curious and not afraid to get involved. There are lots of ways students can get involved in science." Organizations like the National Audubon Society have programs, schools have relationships with universities, and there are afterschool and summer science programs available. Seek out the opportunities and try things that you love.

> "Be curious and not afraid to get involved. There are lots of ways students can get involved in science."

"We are facing a shortage of scientists in our country and in the world just at a time when science is needed more than ever to solve the difficult problems the world is facing." And, the role of scientist is changing, too. "Now, computer scientists are indispensible in figuring out the genomic makeup of all manner of life forms. Even economists and mathematicians are helping biologists figure out why nature works in this way or that." He concludes, "Keep an open mind, follow your passions, and stay curious about nature. That will make you a good scientist."

What Are *Your* Passions?

Deciding on what you want to do when you grow up can seem overwhelming, especially when you are still in school and interested in so many things. Really, though, this is when you should be laying the foundation for future careers—whether it is in the sciences or another field. Try this: Take a clean sheet of paper and list all of the things you *like* to do. For example, do you enjoy playing sports? Hiking? Reading? Writing? Singing songs? Acting? Then, write down what you are interested in learning about. Have you always wanted to travel? See the world? Learn how to knit? Swim with dolphins?

Go through and put a star by the things you are especially interested in. If you had to choose one or two things on your lists, which ones could you *not* live without?

For example, I can't live without books. Books can be found everywhere in my house! I have bookshelves in almost every room. There are books piled next to my bed, the tub, the washing machine, and in my children's playroom. I can pick up a book—nonfiction, fiction, cookbook, and kids' book—any place I go in my house. Seems natural that I would enjoy writing books too, right?

As Robert Mason, and the other scientists in this book have shared, when you are passionate about your career, it is easy to go into work each day. By reflecting on the things you *love* to do and *want* to learn about, you will discover your passions, too. Keep your list somewhere safe. Every few months, or every year, pull it out and add to it or delete things you are no longer interested in. Your passions will grow and evolve as you do. What you truly love, though, will stick with you. Perhaps that will be the basis for an exciting career.

—Colleen

Research Director
James T. Costa, North Carolina

"Young people today often experience the same pressures from our general culture that I experienced when I was in middle school: a cultural stereotype of impractical head-in-the-clouds if not 'mad' scientists," says Dr. James T. Costa, Director of the Highlands Biological Station in North Carolina. "I suspect that most thought that to be curious about nature (astronomy, birds, wildflowers in my case) was pointless, nerdy, not cool." But, it is cool. Being able to follow your passions and having the flexibility to study whatever you want is a great way to spend your life.

Jim's passions have taken him to some amazing places. He has conducted research in the tropics, lectured in the Galapagos Islands, and taught at the University of Oxford in the UK. He is the director of a biological field station and a professor of biology. In his role at the biological station, he plans courses, writes grants, and supervises staff. His job is to take on whatever is needed to keep the facility running well.

"Young people today often experience the same pressures from our general culture that I experienced when I was in middle school: a cultural stereotype of impractical head-in-the-clouds if not 'mad' scientists."

As a professor and scientist, he teaches college courses in biology, conducts research with graduate students, writes papers and books, and presents to groups—both at science meetings and to the public.

When Jim was hired as a research assistant in his sophomore year of college at the State University of New York at Cortland, he learned about the experimental method. He worked with a professor who was studying insect behavior. He says, "I continued working with my professor for the rest of my college career and decided to specialize in that area of biology."

Can Insects Learn?

Insect behavior is fun to study, in part because so many people find them offensive and are repulsed by them. Perhaps one of the most offensive to people is the cockroach. Giant cockroaches make excellent lab specimens because of their size, their availability, and their "ick" factor. They tend to flee from people by scurrying on their legs rather than flying, so they are easier to keep track of during experiments than other insects. In this activity, you will discover whether or not cockroaches can learn their way through a maze. After you have finished with this experiment, enjoy your cockroach as a pet, donate it to a classroom for study, or try designing other experiments and activities for your cockroach to participate in. These are fascinating insects!

Materials

- Giant cockroach with habitat, food, and water
- Foam board
- Clear packing tape
- Clear plastic sheet
- Small cardboard box with a door cut out
- Craft knife
- Stopwatch

Procedure

1. Build two mazes using foam board. One should look like a Y and the other like an X.
   - With an adult's help, cut a base from the foam board in the shape of each maze. (*Note.* It works best to use a craft knife to cut through the top layer of the board. Turn the board over, gently bend it up to make a fold, and cut through on the fold.)
   - Using the same method, cut sides for your maze out of the board.
   - Use clear packing tape to secure your sides to the base and each other.

2. Place the cardboard "house" in one arm of your Y maze.
3. Gently place your cockroach in the bottom of the Y.
4. Cover the top of the maze with the plastic sheet so that you can observe, but your cockroach cannot escape.

5. Watch the cockroach explore the maze until it finds the covered house and hides.

6. Remove the cockroach from its hideout, and return it to the start of the maze.

7. Repeat these steps 5–10 times, depending on how much time you have.

8. You may want to use a stopwatch to time each trial, recording your data to see if the cockroach gets to its hideout more quickly with each trial.

9. Repeat these steps with the X maze, choosing one arm of the X as a starting point and another as the hideout arm where you will place your cardboard house.

10. Answer the following questions:
    • Did your cockroach seem to learn its way through the mazes?
    • Why do you think it did or did not learn?
    • What evidence did you note that supports your findings?
    • How can its ability to learn new things help insects like the cockroach survive in the wild?

11. If you want, save your mazes and try this activity with other insects. You could try having food at the end of your mazes for insects like ants that may be more motivated by food than shade. Compare the results between the different insect species.

Although Jim decided to specialize in biology, he has continued to satisfy his interest in other science disciplines. He says, "In just about all academic disciplines, to earn an advanced degree, it's necessary to become completely expert in one area and make an original contribution to that area. Specializing does not mean that general interests have to be abandoned." He draws regularly on his interests in natural history and the history and philosophy of science in his teaching and research.

Jim continues, "I see myself as a scientist and a communicator of science. As a scientist, I conduct basic research, usually on insect behavioral ecology, and usually with students. As a communicator of science, I teach, give numerous academic and public presentations, and write books and articles."

The science Jim works on is highly dependent on the season of the year. If he is studying insect behavior, he needs to work with live insects in natural populations. For

"I see myself as a scientist and a communicator of science."

example, recently, he spent several hours in the field with a graduate student mapping the distribution of eastern tent caterpillar egg masses on their host trees—the black cherry. "When we are running experiments with caterpillars—one of my favorite study organisms—we must be constantly attentive to them, making sure they don't run out of food, monitoring them in the field, etc. Sometimes this can take many hours of the day."

Tent Caterpillar Trails

Tent caterpillars have been extensively studied because of their interesting and social behavior. Although most caterpillars are solitary, tent caterpillars live in large colonies. They leave pheromone trails to signal food sources to other caterpillars in their colony. This behavior can easily be studied in the classroom or at home. First, though, you will need to go find some caterpillars and food for them.

Materials

- Several tent caterpillars (Different species can be found in favorable weather conditions all over the country. Search the Internet to find species identification information or use a field guide for your area.)
- Food (leaves) for your caterpillars from their host tree
- Cardboard
- Heavy-duty scissors
- Bricks

Procedure

1. Cut your cardboard into a forked trail (one long corridor that branches off into three shorter ones).
2. Raise your maze by putting it up on four bricks standing upright—each supporting a corridor. (If you need more stability, place several bricks upright in the center of the corridors at regular intervals.)
3. Place the caterpillar's food in one of the short corridors.
4. Put a caterpillar at the start of your maze—the beginning of the long corridor.
5. Watch it explore and locate the food.
6. Put the caterpillar back at the start of the maze. Did it find its food again? How quickly?
7. Place several additional caterpillars at the start of the maze. Did they need to explore, or were they able to find the food right away? Why do you think this happened?
8. How can this behavior help tent caterpillars in the wild?

Reflective of his two passions in science, insect social behavior and evolutionary biology, Jim counts the publication of his two books as his greatest accomplishments. *The Other Insect Societies* (Harvard University Press, 2006) and *The Annotated Origin: A Facsimile of the First Edition of On the Origin of Species* (Harvard University Press, 2009) took years of research and writing. He adds, "Science is an empowering way of life. The skills involved in scientific study are incredibly useful in day-to-day life. In addition to a sense of the wonder and beauty of the world, science teaches critical thinking, healthy skepticism, application of rational thought, a sense of cause and effect, and an appreciation of statistics and probability. These are invaluable reasoning skills. Science has a successful track record of figuring things out, and its methodical reasoning approach should not be underestimated. To be a part of that process is, to me, a wonderful thing."

"Science is an empowering way of life. The skills involved in scientific study are incredibly useful in day-to-day life."

Archaeologist
Shary Moose, Washington, DC

About her field, Shary Moose says, "Archaeology is a 'soft science,' not a 'hard science' like physics or chemistry or biology. Our science is more subjective— we ask more *why* questions that don't necessarily have concrete answers. Superstitions, legends, stories that have been handed down, human nature—sometimes people do things that can't be qualified. Like, why is a rabbit's foot lucky? It's not lucky for the rabbit . . ." Archaeologists study the past through what is left behind from other people.

Archaeologists find things that people had years ago. Then, they figure out their stories—how they lived, what they wore, what activities they participated in. "It's like being a detective for stories that happened a long time ago," says Shary. To be a successful archaeologist, you need to be interested in a lot of things. You need to wonder how stuff works, why things are built the way they are, how people think, and you need to enjoy puzzles. You should enjoy looking at a piece of something and wonder what it might look like if it were complete.

"Archaeology is a 'soft science,' not a 'hard science' . . . we ask more <u>why</u> questions that don't necessarily have concrete answers."

Who Found It?

Can you solve this puzzle?

Nadia, Trixie, Benjamin, and Bob are archaeologists. They are each on a different dig (homestead, farmstead, fort, and castle). Each of the archaeologists found an artifact (an arrowhead, a pot, a yoke, and a goblet).

Match each archaeologist with his or her dig and the artifact found.

1. When Trixie was on a castle dig, she knew someone who found a goblet. Now, Trixie is on a different dig.
2. Nadia is on a dig that may have protected Benjamin's location.
3. Benjamin and Bob both like finding arrowheads, but they didn't find one this time.
4. Trixie has watched people on her dig find horseshoes.
5. Nadia's location was less peaceful than Bob's.
6. Benjamin can imagine rulers.
7. A goblet was found at either the farmstead or castle.
8. Benjamin and Trixie have both found arrowheads in the past, but have not found any this time.
9. A yoke was used to guide cattle, and found at either the castle or farmstead.
10. Bob found a pot.
11. A goblet was found at either the castle or homestead.

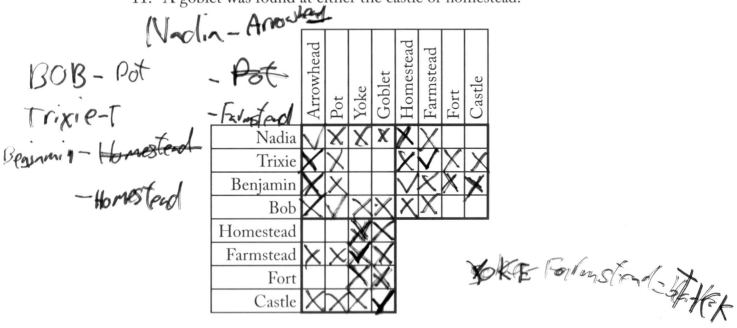

Nadia – Arrowhead

BOB – Pot   – Pot

Trixie – T   – Farmstead

Benjamin – Homestead

– Homestead

YOKE Farmstead –

© Prufrock Press Inc. • Real-Life Science Mysteries

This page may be photocopied or reproduced with permission for single classroom use only.

47

There are two types of archaeology: Academic, which does research-based work, usually through universities, and Cultural Resources Management, which does contract work. Shary does Cultural Resources Management archaeology. She says that it's cool because "you can go anywhere and talk with anyone. Everyone remembers an old building where you're working, or a story from Grandpappy about events that took place near your site." She continues, "It's really quite an experience to discover an artifact from the past that hasn't seen the light of day in X-many years. And here you are, holding it in your hands. I remember finding a coin minted in 1774 and I didn't want to put it down—that's history, the kind you don't get from a book because it's real. It's in your hand, smiling back up at you."

Shary's job is two-fold. She helps find and preserve history, and she educates others about it. Her team will go to a field because someone wants to build a museum. They study the area, dig beneath the surface, and

discover that there was a farmstead there. All of the artifacts are recovered and carefully washed, catalogued, and stored. Then a report is written. The museum gets built, and there is a small display of the archaeology that was done. For example, there is an aircraft museum near Shary that has a small archaeological display. The display is not about aircraft; it's about the farmstead that is under the museum's foundation.

Piecing Together the Past

When archaeologists return from the field, they bring with them the pieces, or artifacts, they find. They put these pieces together the best they can, like a puzzle, to rebuild what was left behind. In this way, they can learn about the people who lived and worked in a location in the past. Often, they find broken ceramics or pottery and piece together vases, tableware, and other things that people of the past used as decorations and tools. The archaeologists can then use these artifacts to learn how long ago the civilization whose people created them lived, how wealthy the civilization was, what types of people lived there, and what materials they had access to. The work can be challenging, but as you will see, once archaeologists hold a complete piece in their hands, very rewarding!

Materials

- A plastic or paper bag containing the pieces of a broken ceramic plate or mug
- A roll of masking tape
- Thick newspaper or plastic to cover your workspace

Procedure

1. Cover a desk, table, or other workstation with thick layers of newspaper or plastic.
2. Spread the contents of your bag on your workstation.
3. Carefully piece together the broken mug or plate. Be careful and pay attention to any rough or sharp edges.
4. Use the masking tape to secure the pieces.
5. When you have finished, display your mug or plate. Was this task easy? Hard? Why?

Archaeology is done in phases. Phase I is the discovery phase. In this phase, archaeologists find out if anything is there. Archaeologists dig lots of small holes all over an area. These holes are placed at regular intervals at intersections like graph paper. They are dug with shovels and the dirt is sifted through a screen. The Phase II assessment phase comes next. In this phase, archaeologists figure out how big the "something" is.

They dig more holes in between the original holes with shovels and sift the dirt again. Finally, Phase III begins. This is the mitigation phase. It is the most complicated. Sometimes, a backhoe comes in to remove the top layers of soil. Other times, things are only partially excavated. "There is a sense of accomplishment you get from helping further the knowledge of history. Plowed fields can turn up long-lost slave sites; golf courses can turn up old cemeteries. Yes, now it's

"Science is not something that is scary. It is not something that only boys are good at. Everyone needs and uses science, sometimes without even knowing they are using it."

just a field, but then . . ."

Archaeology is something anyone can do. There are archaeological societies in just about every state. These societies often sponsor open "digs" where everyday people can join in an excavation.

Shary says to remember, "Science is not something that is scary. It is not something that only boys are good at. Everyone needs and uses science, sometimes without even knowing they are using it. And, the more science you know and understand, the better you'll be able to learn about and appreciate the world around you."

Hydrogeologist
Ben Daigneau, Arizona

Ben Daigneau thought he would be a teacher when he started college. But as he took classes, he slowly fell in love with geology. Now he works as a hydrogeologist in Arizona. "Just about every piece of dirt and every rock has an interesting story to tell," he says. "I studied geology in college, as there was not much specialization available at my school, and have learned a lot about hydrogeology on the job."

Hydrogeology is a subfield of geology. It focuses on groundwater as opposed to surface water like rivers and streams. "It's much easier to make the distinction between ground and surface water in Arizona, where we find it at hundreds of feet below the surface, compared to other parts of the country where water is very close to the surface and the two types are linked." Hydrogeology centers on how water moves under the surface of the Earth.

Groundwater is very important to people and the environment. Many people use groundwater every day without even realizing it. It is used for drinking, to irrigate crops, and more. A hydrogeologist finds water. He or she determines the quantity and quality of the water, as well as the usage rights. In the desert, where Ben works, water allocation is watched carefully. He helps to figure out how much a community or manufacturer will need and helps them contact the state to get rights to use it.

Groundwater and the Water Cycle

Remember that groundwater is extremely important to life and to the water cycle. All plants need water to grow. All animals—including humans—need water to live. The water supply on Earth is constantly reestablishing itself through the water cycle. Water from the world's oceans, lakes, rivers, and other water sources evaporates as a result of heat from the sun and rises into the air, condensing into clouds, then falls back down to the Earth as precipitation; is absorbed into the soil as groundwater, which is used by plants and animals; evaporates and condenses into more clouds, then falls again to the Earth as precipitation. Create your own groundwater/water cycle model now.

Materials

- Clear plastic cup
- Plastic wrap
- Aquarium gravel
- Potting soil
- Spray bottle
- Water
- Cress or other quick-growing seeds
- Rubber band
- Tape

Procedure

1. Fill your spray bottle with water.
2. Place an inch to an inch and a half of gravel at the bottom of your cup.
3. Fill the cup with potting soil, leaving an inch of space at the top.
4. Plant your seeds in the soil according to the seed packet's instructions.
5. Water liberally by spraying the spray bottle into the cup, on the soil, and on the inner sides of the cup.
6. Watch through the outer sides of the cup as the water trickles down through the soil and into the gravel. This water is your groundwater. The groundwater will be used by the seeds as they grow.
7. Cover the cup tightly with plastic wrap, securing with either a rubber band or tape.
8. Place the cup in a window that gets a lot of sunlight.

9. Watch the water cycle over the next few days—the sides of your cup will get foggy as the water evaporates and condenses. This fogginess represents the "clouds" we see in the sky. As the clouds become heavy with water, they will "rain" back down into the soil and become groundwater again for your seeds.

Most of the time, groundwater is clean, but it can become contaminated if people are careless. Ben also must do environmental work. He says, "If an industry contaminates the groundwater, we help to find out how to clean it up." He will discover what pollutant was released, how much, and if it is still leaching into the groundwater.

One of the things Ben enjoys most about his job is the satisfaction he feels after installing a well. "Trying to figure out what's happening in a 10-foot diameter hole that descends 750 feet below the surface is hard to do. It's hard on tools, and the unexpected always seems to happen." The water in a well is pumped up from an aquifer. An aquifer is an area below the surface that holds groundwater. Wells pump groundwater from that aquifer and into the places it will be used.

Groundwater Contamination

Groundwater fills the cracks and spaces between rocks, sand, and gravel in the ground. It is stored there, and moves as it is used by plants and animals. Wells can be dug to tap into this supply and bring fresh water to the surface for human use. Aquifers, the locations underground that store groundwater, can be replenished through precipitation. They also can be contaminated through human carelessness. When contamination occurs, the water becomes unsafe and cannot be used by humans and other organisms.

Materials

- Clear plastic drinking cup
- Aquarium gravel
- Sand
- A bottle of water
- A spray bottle filled with water
- Food coloring

Procedure

1. Fill the cup with gravel about a third of the way to the top.
2. Add sand to another third of the cup so that you are left with ⅓ gravel, ⅓ sand, and ⅓ space.
3. Pour water from the bottle slowly into the cup, observing the way in which the water fills in the spaces between gravel and sand particles. Fill the cup until the water is just below the sand layer. The top of the water is called the water table. The water below this is called the saturation zone.

4. Answer the following questions:
   - Did the water move faster through the gravel or the sand?
   - Why?

5. Sprinkle some food coloring on top of the sand to represent a contaminant.
6. Use your spray bottle to "rain" on top of the contaminated ground.
7. Answer the following questions:
   - What happens to your groundwater as rain pours onto the contaminated "Earth?"
   - Why is it so important for humans to be careful as they transport chemicals or other pollutants across the land?
   - How does this experiment demonstrate the possibilities of pesticide contamination?

Ben concludes, "I think the biggest impact that my field can have is to help strike the balance between the health of the people and the health of the planet." He adds that "geology stretches your imagination from the very small to the very large. There are rock formations that take a day to form because a landslide occurs, and there are rock formations that take millions of years to form. If you look at a mountain range, you see individual rivers. Those rivers take the mountain down, one grain of sand at a time. Then, you imagine how it got there and picture it being uplifted when a continent collided with another one. I could get lost in that stuff for days."

"Geology stretches your imagination from the very small to the very large. There are rock formations that take a day to form because a landslide occurs, and there are rock formations that take millions of years to form. If you look at a mountain range, you see individual rivers. Those rivers take the mountain down, one grain of sand at a time."

Landscape Architect
Tony Colini, Ohio

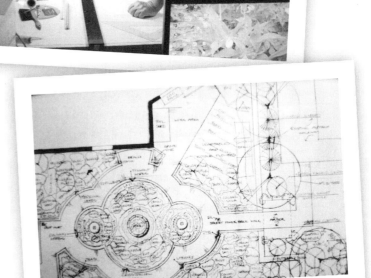

Although it may not seem like it at first glance, Tony Colini uses science every day in his job as owner of Sweetbay Gardens in Ohio and as a landscape architect. The focus of his landscape work is developing plans, then building, installing, planting, and maintaining landscapes. He says that "everything [he does] is connected to science." The science used in landscape design encompasses physical, Earth, and life sciences.

In fact, landscape architecture is a field in which art and science intersect. No matter how beautiful a design is, if you plant sun-loving species in a location that experiences an abundance of wet shade, nothing will grow. A landscape architect is creating living art. Tony says that the biggest motivation he has is "the beauty created for others to enjoy." He especially enjoys planning a project on paper and then following it through to a finished, and gorgeous, end result.

A landscape architect is creating living art.

Pizza Gardening

Now it is your turn to design and plant a beautiful and functional garden. For this activity, you will learn how to grow everything (well, almost everything!) to make a delicious pizza.

Materials

- Large circular deck planter or ground plot in a sunny location
- Potting soil
- Seeds or seedlings: basil, oregano, parsley, thyme, Roma tomato, and pepper
- Graph paper
- Pencil
- Yarn
- Garden stakes
- Permanent marker

Procedure

1. Draw your garden plan on a piece of graph paper.
   - Draw a circle and divide it into six wedges.
   - Decide what wedge will hold what plant. You may want to think about the color, texture, and size of your plants. Which order will look the best?

2. Using yarn, divide your plot or container into sixths.

3. Plant your seeds or seedlings in the pizza wedges, according to your design.
4. Follow your seed packet or garden center instructions for caring for your plants throughout their growing season.
5. When it is time to harvest your plants, make pizza according to the recipe below.

Pizza Garden Pizza

Note. This recipe requires adult assistance.

Ingredients

- Store-bought whole wheat pizza crust
- 6–8 tomatoes
- 2 tablespoons of chopped basil
- 2 tablespoons of chopped oregano
- 1 tablespoon of thyme
- 2 tablespoons of parsley
- 1 clove of minced garlic
- 1 teaspoon of salt
- 1/2 teaspoon of pepper
- Chopped pizza garden peppers
- Mozzarella cheese

Directions

1. Follow directions on the store-bought pizza crust to determine if pre-cooking is required.
2. Put tomatoes in a pot of boiling water for 30 seconds, scoop them out with a slotted spoon, and drop into ice water.
3. When the tomatoes are cool, use a paring knife to remove skins and cores.
4. Cut the tomatoes in lengthwise quarters and remove the seeds; then chop them in a food processor.
5. Put the chopped tomatoes, basil, oregano, thyme, parsley, garlic, salt, and pepper in a pot.
6. Simmer the sauce over medium-low heat for half an hour.
7. Spread the sauce on the pizza crust, put a thick layer of cheese over the sauce, and add chopped peppers.
8. Bake your pizza according to the directions on the crust until cheese is bubbly and slightly browned.
9. Enjoy!

Knowing where, when, and how to plant various species of native plants is essential to landscape architects. So is an understanding of invasive species and how to get rid of them. An invasive species is a plant that is not native to an area in which it is now growing. Invasive plants can take over areas from native plants—those that are supposed to be there.

A landscape architect must be able to prep the soil for planting. Tony must keep in mind the physical needs of each plant type he plans to use. Does the plant require sun? Partial sun? Shade? How about moisture? Or soil conditions? Should the soil be sandy? Contain clay? How much? Tony admits to being surprised about all of the knowledge required in his field. There are so many facets.

On top of all of the challenges faced in the field while designing and installing landscapes, there are other sciences involved in the day-to-day operation of Tony's nursery. To properly grow and experiment with plants, he must have an understanding of biology, chemistry, and physics. He must know about the environment and what it requires to stay healthy. He also needs to understand entomology so he can determine which insects

are threats to which plants and how to protect them from damage.

A nursery owner and operator should have university training in horticulture to understand the physiology of plants. This especially comes in handy when growing plants for nursery stock—to use in landscape designs or to sell for others to use.

Plants can be grown in several ways. They can grow when their seeds are planted. Some new plants can be grown by planting cuttings from a parent plant. Others can be grafted. Grafting is when tissues from one plant are forced to join together with tissues from another plant. Grafting can also be used to form new plants.

Grafting Bean Plants

When a plant gets a cut, like a human, it will heal over in time. When a horticulturist grafts plants, he or she is taking advantage of the plants' ability to heal themselves. Sometimes, grafting is used to create new species, and sometimes it is used to make a plant healthier by joining an unhealthy plant with a healthy one. In this activity, you will join two different bean species together and watch them grow into one plant.

Materials

- Two different types of bean plants, each about a foot tall
- Kitchen paring knife
- Electrical tape
- String

Procedure

1. Put the two plants next to each other and find a spot where their main stems touch comfortably.
2. Pare the stems at this point just enough to expose the inside of the stems.
3. Hold the stems together at their cuts and wrap tightly with electrical tape.
4. Tie some string around the stems right below and above the graft for added support.
5. Watch the plants closely, keeping them watered and pruned, for about a week. When you notice that they are both doing well, cut off the top of one plant and the bottom of the other.
6. Watch your plant for several more weeks. How is it doing?

Whether it involves creating new plants, clearing invasive species from an area and reintroducing native species, or designing and installing a new landscape, the job of a landscape architect is cool! There are so many facets to it as science, nature, and art intersect to create beauty in the natural world. Tony concludes, "We are stewards of the Earth—we should respect it, enjoy it, and preserve it for future generations."

Name: _____   Date: _____

Mechanical Project Engineer
Doug Barnes, Ohio

Doug Barnes has always been interested in learning how things worked. Growing up, he often helped fix things around the house or the family cars—just to see what made them go. He also was interested in architecture: "When I was younger, I used to fill notebooks with sketches of skyscrapers as if I was an architect." Doug later spent time with an architect and learned what he did all day.

"When I was younger, I used to fill notebooks with sketches of skyscrapers as if I was an architect."

Now, he combines his love of architecture and his fascination with how things work in his job. He says, "I am a mechanical project engineer for an MEP (mechanical, electrical, plumbing) consulting firm. I design heating, cooling, and plumbing systems for all types of commercial and institutional buildings. I typically work as a consultant for an architect who is designing hospitals, laboratories, or museums."

Mechanical engineering is a field that crosses over into the three main science domains. "On the physical side, we must understand the properties of thermodynamics and fluid dynamics to correctly design a building. On the Earth side, we deal with both the materials that objects are made of and the 'green' aspect of creating a building in harmony with its surroundings. On the life side, we need to understand the physiology of humans to make both a comfortable and useful space. This creates a unique balance between the buildings we help create and the people that use them."

Thermodynamic Treats

Did you know that it takes science to make ice cream? Doug uses thermodynamics in his job of designing heating and cooling systems in buildings. In this activity, you will use thermodynamics to make yourself a tasty treat! How? Heat energy from the milk mixture will flow into the ice and salt mixture, and vice versa, until the two are similar in temperature. By adding the salt to the ice, you lower the freezing point of the ice.

The second law of thermodynamics, the Law of Entropy, explains why your milk mixture becomes similar in temperature to the ice brine. This law explains that energy from objects in the universe will disperse, or spread out, if it is not kept from doing so. The nature of energy is to eventually even out with other energy molecules around it. So, a pan eventually cools when taken off a heat source, and its fast-moving energy slows to the same speed as the energy moving in the room-temperature air. Like that pan, the energy in the cold ice-brine mixture speeds up, while the molecules in the milk mixture slow down, until they reach the same speed—milk mixture and ice-brine—and are the same temperature.

Materials

- 1 cup of milk
- 1 cup of half and half
- ½ a cup of sugar
- 1 teaspoon of vanilla
- 1 large zip-top baggie
- 1 small zip-top baggie
- Ice
- Rock salt
- Spoon
- Toppings

Procedure

1. Mix the milk, half and half, sugar, and vanilla in the small zip-top bag.
2. Place the small zip-top bag inside the large zip-top bag.
3. Put ½ to 1 cup of rock salt in the large zip-top bag next to the small zip-top bag and fill with ice.
4. Make sure both bags are tightly sealed.
5. Shake the bags as hard as you can for 10–15 minutes.
6. Pull the small bag out of the large bag.

7. Toss some sprinkles or chopped up cookies into the small bag, and dig in with a spoon! A plastic baggie sundae. Yum!

A typical day for Doug starts around 7:30 a.m. with meetings to help him and the other engineers brush up on the latest technology or design guidelines. He works with others on a team, so there are e-mails and phone calls to be taken care of. Sometimes, he's out on a construction site reviewing the installation of the mechanical systems. He notes, "The majority of [design work] is done on a computer using Computer Aided Drafting (CAD) software. I spend most of my day using a computer either for design or documentation."

When designing mechanical systems for new buildings, Doug might need to calculate the amount of heat gain or loss. "This involves defining the materials used to construct the building, determining the amount of heat transfer from convection, conduction, and radiation, and then designing a heating or cooling system to transfer that heat in or out of the building." He may need to determine how surrounding wind patterns will impact the cleanliness of the air going into a building. "This involves modeling the effect the building has on the surrounding landscape, finding the impact of traffic to the air quality, and determining the best location for fresh air intake."

Experiencing Radiation, Conduction, and Convection

Heat is important to humans. We are warm-blooded and need to maintain a healthy range in our body temperatures. In order to maintain our body temperatures, we need people who understand radiation, conduction, and convection, or heat transfer, to create heating and cooling systems for the places in which we live. In this activity, you will learn the basic differences between the ways in which heat is transferred.

Materials

- An outside wall heated by the sun
- Candle
- Lighter or matches
- Scissors
- Paper
- Tape
- Yarn

Procedure

1. Stand outside in a shady location.
2. Think about how you feel. Is it hot? Cool? Do you feel your body absorbing heat from the sun?
3. Move to a sunny location near a wall.
4. Again, think about what you feel. Is it hot? Cool? Do you feel your body absorbing heat from the sun?
5. You are experiencing radiation. This is the method by which the sun's energy reaches Earth. Energy travels in rays and we feel these rays touching our body as the rays warm our body's surface.
6. Touch your cheeks with the palms of your hands.
7. How warm or cool do your hands feel on your cheeks?
8. Place your palms on the wall that has been heated in the sun. Keep them there until your palms have absorbed the heat and feel warmer than before.
9. Feel your cheeks again. What is the difference in temperature from when you rested your palms on your cheeks before? Colder? Warmer?
10. In this case, you were feeling conduction. This is the direct transfer of energy by collision. The heat energy that was in

the wall collided with your hands and transferred heat to the palms, which you then transferred to your cheeks.

11. Now, cut your paper into a spiral.
12. Tape the yarn to the center of your paper spiral.
13. Carefully, and with adult supervision, light your candle and hold the paper spiral directly over the flame.
14. Hold the paper spiral as still as you can. After a few minutes, watch it spin.
15. This is convection. Heat energy moves up from the flame and displaces the air above it. This causes the paper spiral to spin.

Doug says that most people don't realize the brainpower and science that goes into designing and building structures in today's society. One of his biggest motivations is the knowledge that the buildings he had a hand in designing are being used to help other people. He worked on the renovation of the Cleveland Museum of Art and was fascinated to know that this building, which has been around since 1916, might be around for another hundred years, with his contribution helping keep it strong.

He concludes, "One thing to remember is that those who make a career in a scientific field will never stop learning. Even now, I learn from the engineers around me who have more experience. At times, it can be a struggle, but at the same time, it keeps you on your toes and makes for a rewarding and fascinating career."

"Most people don't realize the brainpower and science that goes into designing and building structures in today's society."

Materials Scientist
Joseph V. Ryan, Washington State

Imagine what it would be like to spend your day trying to find solutions to some of the United States' most important scientific problems: problems related to energy, the environment, national security, and more. Joe Ryan, senior scientist at the Pacific National Laboratory in Washington state, can—and does! Every day!

"As a materials scientist, I use the periodic table as a toolbox to design and make new materials that can do new things. Most of my work stems from designing new storage forms for nuclear waste. Nuclear waste disposal is a hard problem . . . the waste has to be put into a form where it will be stable for up to a million years! Right now, we turn the waste into a really durable glass and are studying just how durable it is. When you think about it, this is really hard to do . . . if a material doesn't change much over a millennium, how on Earth do you study how it *does* change?"

Imagine what it would be like to spend your day trying to find solutions to some of the United States' most important scientific problems.

Working with glass isn't something Joe reserves for his time on the job, though. "I'm a glassblower and love to make big multicolored squiggly glass sculptures to have around my home," Joe says. He believes that making things out of glass is a great way to get kids involved in science.

"It's really hot, there's fire involved, and glass occasionally crashes and shatters on the floor." Seriously, though, the science behind blowing glass for art is just as critical as using glass for other purposes. "The viscosity (gooey-ness) of the glass has to be just right . . . it can't get too runny too quickly. Getting the colors right requires the perfect chemistry of metal ions in the glass. And I love to play with the fact that glass can be cold enough to crack on the surface, but molten on the inside . . . it makes really neat patterns!"

Sugar Glass

Although you can't turn your classroom into a glassblowing studio, you can experiment with the "glass" of Hollywood. Have you ever seen someone fall through a window or glass door in a movie? How about an actor breaking a bottle over another actor's head? If so, you've seen sugar glass.

Sugar glass is a prop for Hollywood stunts because it looks like real glass but is softer, and not as sharp. Try making your own sheet of sugar glass. You can make clear glass or experiment with some food coloring at the last minute. Mmmmm . . . edible stained glass windows!

Materials

- Heavy, deep saucepan
- 2 cups of water
- 1 cup of corn syrup
- 3 ½ cups of sugar
- ¼ teaspoon of cream of tartar
- Food coloring
- Candy thermometer
- Vegetable oil
- Baking sheet with shallow sides
- Butter knife or toothpick

Procedure

1. Oil your baking sheet completely. Make sure that you cover the bottom and the sides.
2. Bring the water, corn syrup, cream of tartar, and sugar to a rapid boil in the saucepan.
3. Continue boiling your mixture until the candy thermometer shows 300 degrees. (*Note.* This could take up to an hour, boiling most of the liquid off. Your mixture should be very thick by the time it reaches this temperature.)
4. Pour the mixture into your oiled baking pan.
5. If you want to, drop some food coloring into the mixture in the pan and swirl it around with a toothpick or butter knife.
6. Let cool completely.
7. Carefully pop the mixture out of the mold.
8. You now have a glass window—just like the kind that Hollywood stars fall through!

In school, Joe liked physics and Earth science best. He once thought he would be a meteorologist, and continues to observe the weather as a hobby. Really, though, all sciences were interesting to him. And now, that eclectic love of science helps him out. "There are so many avenues to materials science that someone who was interested in any science (biology, chemistry, physics, engineering, etc.) could be good at it. You just have to have a knack for solving problems," he says.

One of his favorite experiences in school was being a part of a program called Odyssey of the Mind where he had to build a machine that could do all kinds of tasks and was powered by mousetraps. "I also did experiments in chemistry at home, trying to find a better plant food. My mother always wondered why her plants never did very well . . . perhaps pickle juice mixed with paint thinner isn't a very good fertilizer!"

> "My advice to young people is to stay curious . . . keep asking why and finding out the reasons behind the way the world works. Don't just acquire knowledge from Wikipedia or textbooks—try it out!"

He shares, "My advice to young people is to stay curious . . . keep asking why and finding out the reasons behind the way the world works. Don't just acquire knowledge from Wikipedia or textbooks—try it out! There will come a day when no one on the planet has the answer . . . yet. Knowing how to get involved and find it is what will make you a good scientist."

Design a Better . . .

Scientists solve problems by experimenting with materials. Like Joe, they use chemicals, minerals, and compounds, but they also use everyday materials. The program Joe mentioned, Odyssey of the Mind, gives kids a chance to invent and test their inventions. (Check out the Odyssey of the Mind website to learn more about the program. You can find it at: http://www.odysseyofthemind.com) Odyssey of the Mind participants solve problems and try to come up with ways to make the world a better place. You can try this, too.

Come up with a problem to solve. Some suggestions include:
- How to design boats that can hold incredible weights.
- How to design a car that will protect passengers during a collision.
- How to make houses safer during hurricanes.
- How to build structurally sound buildings along fault lines.

Use materials that you can find around the house or classroom. Examples include:
- Tape
- Straws
- Craft sticks
- Paper
- Index cards
- String
- Foil
- Yarn
- Egg cartons
- Boxes
- Mousetraps

Procedure

1. Choose your problem.
2. Choose your materials.
3. Build your improved product prototype.
4. Test it. For example, if you are building a house that can withstand a hurricane, set up the house and direct a fan on it. Does it hold up?
5. Ask yourself, "How can I make my next one work even better?"
6. Try it again, tweaking your prototype.
7. Keep experimenting!

Joe says, "The coolest part of my job is inventing or discovering something totally new. This happens more often than you'd think, and is an incredible feeling when it does. Usually the discoveries are small, advancing science another step. Occasionally, though, you get to be a part of something that generates a patent or puts forth a new scientific theory. I have a couple of patents and was fortunate to publish an article in a very prestigious journal. I've also come up with some ideas that might make nuclear waste storage better for future generations."

About his motivation, he notes, "You'd think the biggest motivating factor would be inventing something to change the world and benefit mankind, but it's not. It's really a lot simpler than that: I just like to find out how the world works. Physical science is like a puzzle and the more we know, the more we can use it to solve problems in the future leading to even more understanding and more pieces of the puzzle."

He concludes, "Science has gotten more and more important over the history of mankind, leading to innovations that have shaped our world. It is amazingly exciting to be on the forefront of this exploration and to be a part of the solutions to today's problems."

Forensic Scientist
Rebekah Herrick, Vermont

When Rebekah Herrick was in school, she remembers being fascinated by the interconnectedness of all of the different types of science. "Biology needs chemistry to be fully explained," she says. "Likewise, within biology, which is a huge field, there are many different parts that are all related. For instance, the way cells work controls the way bacteria and viruses affect people. I guess I was fascinated by how vast and intertwined all of the different fields of science are." To do her job, however, she must stay focused. It is important to pay close attention to details because people's lives depend on her job.

Rebekah is a forensic scientist. She works as a DNA analyst for the Vermont State Forensics Lab. She says, "Because people's lives depend on our work, there is no room for mistakes; my work is always double checked and sometimes triple checked. You also need to have steady hands because much of what I do is fine detail work."

Her work focuses on processing samples collected from convicted criminals.

"I was fascinated by how vast and intertwined all of the different fields of science are."

In many states, people who are convicted of, or under investigation for, a crime must submit a DNA sample to be included in a database. She is the one who processes those samples to be added to the database. Other analysts process samples from evidence found at crime scenes. "These samples are usually collected and brought to the lab by police officers. Once an analyst has developed the profile from the evidence, it can be compared to the database of profiles that I develop. If we get a match, then we can give the police the name of the offender to help their investigation."

Rebekah continues, "Forensics work doesn't often have individual accomplishments. It's really a team effort. Since I started at the lab, we've assisted in cold murder cases, as well as a few active ones. While the CODIS database may play a role in that, without my coworkers processing the samples that the police bring us, no progress would be made."

> "Forensics work doesn't often have individual accomplishments. It's really a team effort."

A typical day includes extracting DNA from cells. These are usually buccal swabs, which are skin cells from the inside of a person's cheek. "Those cells are lysed, or broken apart, using chemicals. Then, all the contents of the cell (proteins, mitochondria, DNA, etc. . . .) are all floating loose. I use specially designed filters and buffers that trap the DNA and let all of the other things flow through."

Extracting DNA

Your body gets its instructions for growth from the DNA that is present in the nucleus of every cell. Chromosomes are formed from DNA. These contain the information for building more cells. DNA determines a person's hair color, height, eye color, and just about everything about his or her body. Every living thing has DNA that tells it how to grow. In this activity, you will learn how to extract DNA from a living thing—a bean.

Materials

- Blender
- Strainer
- Glass bowl
- Glass baby food jars
- Rubbing alcohol
- Dried pinto beans
- Salt
- Cold water
- Dish detergent
- Meat tenderizer
- Wooden toothpick
- Wooden spoon
- Wooden craft stick

Procedure

1. Put ½ a cup of beans, ⅛ teaspoon of salt, and 1 cup of cold water into the blender. Blend on high for 30 seconds so that the bean cells are separated.
2. Pour your bean mixture through a strainer into your glass bowl.
3. Mix in 2 tablespoons of dish detergent with the spoon and let sit for 15 minutes. This separates the cell membrane from the nucleus where DNA is found.
4. Pour your mixture into your baby food jars, each only about ¼ to ⅓ full.
5. Add a small pinch of tenderizer to each jar and stir with a craft stick. The tenderizer is an enzyme and will cut the protein that binds and protects the DNA in the nucleus of the cell.
6. Pick up a baby food jar, tilt it, and *slowly* add rubbing alcohol so it forms a layer on the top of the bean mixture. Your alcohol layer should be about as thick as your bean mixture.

7. Look closely at where the mixture and alcohol meet. You should see a white stringy substance. The substance is tangled clumps of bean DNA. Normally, DNA stays dissolved in water, but the salt you added to your mixture makes it show up when it comes into contact with the alcohol.

8. If you want, you can pull the bean DNA out with a wooden toothpick.

The coolest part of Rebekah's job is helping to solve crimes. "It's not like a TV show," she says. "Day to day, it's a lot like working in any other science lab. But helping to solve a murder is pretty cool." She adds that she hopes nobody ever has to deal with her or her coworkers because that means that you have been the victim of a crime. "However, for people who have been victimized, we make a big difference. We can track down a burglar using blood found at the scene. We can help bring a criminal to justice for a murder that happened 20 years ago. And for those victims, our work is very important."

For students interested in a future career in forensics, Rebekah says that it is important to make good choices. "Stay in school, and don't do drugs," she says. You hear it all the time, and it is true. "Many forensics labs have very detailed background checks of their potential employees. You have to have a really clean record to work in law enforcement, even as a civilian." Other than that, she says to explore your surroundings. "Science is a short word covering a vast realm of possibilities. And by the time students in middle and high school right now graduate college, I bet there will be science jobs available that don't even exist yet—some of them in forensics!"

"Science is a short word covering a vast realm of possibilities. And by the time students in middle and high school right now graduate college, I bet there will be science jobs available that don't even exist yet—some of them in forensics!"

Biophysicist
Niko Grigorieff, Massachusetts

Amyloid beta protein (Abeta)

When Niko Grigorieff was a kid, he approached his science classes as puzzle-solving sessions. He enjoyed hands-on activities, such as making electricity with a homemade generator or making his own hydrogen balloon with hydrochloric acid and zinc.

Taking the fun from classroom to home, he found unique answers to problems he faced. Have you ever had a parent complain about your loud music? When Niko's mom tried to turn off his stereo, she was surprised to hear the music continue after cutting off the electricity. Niko had created his own electrical inverter using a car battery!

Construct a Simple Reading Lamp

Now it is your turn to solve the mystery of electrical circuitry like Niko did when he was a kid. With this simple circuit and a few additional materials, you will be able to create a small book light to use the next time you read in bed at night!

Materials

- Coated wire
- 3-volt watch battery
- Small LED bulb
- Small binder clip
- Large binder clip
- Wire hanger
- Wire strippers
- Wire cutters
- Pliers
- Hot glue gun
- Book

Procedure

1. Prepare the bulb:
   - Cut two pieces of wire, about 2 inches long.
   - Use the wire strippers to strip a small amount of plastic from either end of each wire.
   - Using your hot glue gun (adult supervision required), attach one end of one wire to the base of the bulb.
   - Attach an end of the other wire to the side of the bulb with hot glue.
   - You now have a bulb with wires attached.

2. Prepare the battery:
   - Hot glue one of the wires coming from the bulb to the positive side of the battery.

3. Prepare the hanger:
   - Have an adult cut the hook off of the wire hanger.
   - Have the adult use pliers to straighten the hanger.
   - Using the pliers, have the adult pinch one end of the hanger around the handle of the large binder clip.

- Hot glue the hanger and binder clip together at a 90-degree angle so that they won't slip apart—this may take a lot of hot glue.
- Bend the hanger at about a 45-degree angle on the other end.
- Attach the small binder clip to the other end of the hanger.

4. Put it all together:
   - Clamp the large binder clip to a book so that the curve of the hanger is above the pages.
   - Hold the unattached wire coming from the LED light to the negative end of the battery. The wires should be attached to each end of the battery, forming a circuit and making the bulb light up.
   - Clamp the battery, wires, and light in the small binder clip so that the light hangs over your book.

Now, Niko is Dr. Niko Grigorieff, a biophysicist and professor at Brandeis University in Waltham, MA. In college, he studied physics, especially semiconductors that are used to build lasers. Instead of continuing to study high-speed optical networks, Niko turned his interest to biology. He applied his use of the electron microscope to study cells of living things. Now, he walks a scientific line between life science, physical science, and computer science.

By using the electron microscope to see deep inside cells, he hopes to see the atomic details of the molecules that come together to form living cells. Electron microscopes can magnify things several hundred thousand times.

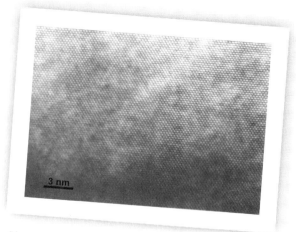

Electron microscope image of a semiconductor crystal

Comparing Images

It may be hard to imagine the difference between images seen with an electron microscope and an optical microscope. An optical microscope shines light through an object that rests on its stage. It can magnify small things like cells and insects up to about one thousand times. Electron microscopes use electrons to magnify images. They send a charge through small things to light them up for magnification. Because electrons have wavelengths that are much shorter than visible light waves, they can achieve magnification of up to one million times.

Materials

- Optical microscope
- Prepared slides of plant cells
- Prepared slides of cheek cells
- Photos from this book or the Internet of electron microscope images
- Textbook, poster, or Internet resource

Procedure

1. Use your microscope to look at images of plant cells and cheek cells.
2. Try to identify the different parts of each cell and draw what you see.
3. Label your diagrams, using a textbook, poster, or Internet resource that helps you identify the parts of plant and human cells.
4. Now, look at the images from the electron microscope. You can do an Internet search for plant and cheek cell images using this type of microscope, or you can look at the images of the tobacco mosaic virus (TMV) that affects the cells of the tobacco plant or the rotavirus (RV) images. Remember that viruses cannot be seen with the naked eye. These viruses affect individual cells and are therefore unable to be seen with the microscope you are currently using.
5. Compare your diagrams of cells with the images of viruses that affect cells.

Niko says that the coolest part of his job is seeing tiny molecules and how they come together like "parts of a machine to perform their function." He says that "rotavirus looks like a ball with 60 spikes." Rotavirus causes vomiting and diarrhea in infants and children. "It has three layers that are shed one after another when the virus enters a cell. On the inside, it carries the genes that tell the cell how to make a new virus. Realizing how the virus tricks the cell to make it produce more virus, even though the virus will eventually kill the cell, is fascinating and scary at the same time." Rotavirus is like something you might see in a science fiction movie.

But understanding viruses at their atomic level can have an incredible impact. For example, knowing how Alzheimer's filaments (chain-like series of cells) form can help scientists discover how to cure this disease. Niko notes, "Scientific research is a tough business that is certainly not for everyone." He adds, "Most of us are scientists in one way or another because we use scientific methods to figure out problems." If you like observation, logical thinking, troubleshooting, and figuring things out when others have walked away, "science could become the greatest joy in your life."

Electron microscope image of tobacco mosaic virus.

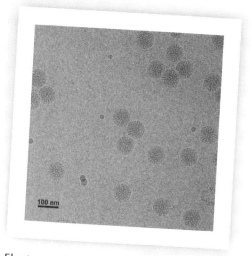

Electron microscope image of rotaviruses

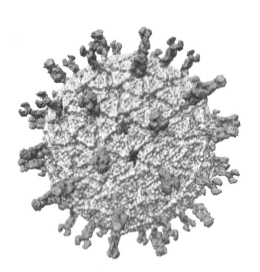

If you like observation, logical thinking, troubleshooting, and figuring things out when others have walked away, "science could become the greatest joy in your life."

Cardiothoracic Surgeon
Patrick Ryan, Jr.
Washington State

A typical day for Dr. Patrick Ryan, Jr., M.D., includes a meeting at 7 a.m. to discuss program and hospital issues at the Providence Regional Medical Center where he works. Most days, he operates on heart and lung patients. These operations include bypass surgery to improve blood supply to the heart and repair or replace diseased valves. He may remove lung tumors. He also may repair collapsed lungs and drain lung infections.

Knowing human physiology is important to Patrick's job. He uses that knowledge every day in his work. "I rearrange body parts to make the heart function better. I adjust medications to help facilitate recovery. I look at blood tests and x-rays to monitor recovery and head off complications."

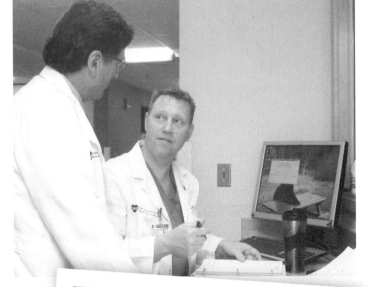

Knowing human physiology is important to Patrick's job.

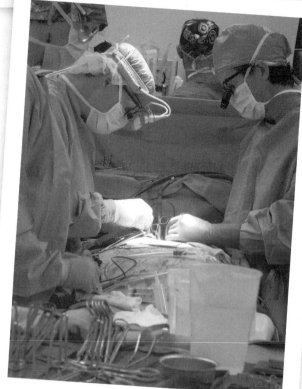

Observing Blood Flow

Blood moves to and from the heart in a system called circulation. Blood flows into the heart to receive oxygen, and the oxygenated blood flows back into the body, bringing oxygen-saturated blood to the organs. This keeps the body's temperature regulated and helps muscles work effectively. In this activity, you will be able to see how blood moves through capillaries, veins, and arteries.

Materials

- Live frog
- Wet cloth
- Microscope

Procedure

1. Wrap a frog carefully in a wet cloth and hold it gently, but securely.
2. Place one of the frog's hind feet on the stage of your microscope and spread its toes.
3. Turn the microscope's light on.
4. Focus your eyepiece on the webbing between the frog's toes.
5. You should be able to see the frog's capillaries. Observe the flow of blood through those capillaries, veins, and arteries.

It is important for a heart surgeon to be confident. He needs to be comfortable in intense situations. When someone's life is at stake, a cardiothoracic surgeon must be able to stay calm and focused. Patrick says he has been surprised at "the intense sense of commitment to my patients and practice [I have] developed over time. I guess I did not realize how strong those feelings can be and how it [would affect] me when things don't go as expected."

Patrick has had an interest in the life sciences since high school. Now he works to understand the workings of human anatomy. "When I was younger, I wanted to be an engineer like my dad. I changed my mind after taking anatomy and physiology in high school. We got to dissect a cat!" It may have been the hands-on science that led him to his work, but a desire to improve the lives of fellow humans has made him the surgeon he is today.

Heartbeats

Long ago, doctors would press their ears to their patients' chests to listen to their heartbeats. In 1816, French doctor René Théophile Hyacinthe Laënnec experimented by using a paper tube to listen to a patient's heartbeat. Using this tube, he realized that the sound of the heart could be isolated and amplified. This made heart and chest exams easier to interpret.

Modern stethoscopes have a bell-shaped device on the end with a plastic diaphragm connected to plastic tubing. The tubes lead to two earpieces. The bell is placed on a patient's chest or back, and a doctor can listen through the earpieces to the amplified sound traveling through the tube.

Materials

- Stethoscope
- Alcohol
- Cotton balls
- Watch with a second hand

Procedure

1. Wipe the earpieces of your stethoscope with an alcohol-soaked cotton ball.
2. Place the earpieces in your ears.
3. Place the bell of the stethoscope onto a friend's chest.
4. Listen for heart sounds.
5. Identify the first sound. This is the ventricular contraction, or systole.
6. Listen for the second sound. This is the ventricular relaxation, or diastole.
7. How much time passed between the two sounds?
8. Time the interval between the second sound and the next first sound.
9. After five of these intervals, you can estimate the average time the heart is at rest each minute.

© Prufrock Press Inc. • Real-Life Science Mysteries

This page may be photocopied or reproduced with permission for single classroom use only.

86

A piece of advice Patrick has for young people who may want to get into cardiothoracic medicine is to volunteer and develop a commitment to service. This can help strengthen that sense of commitment to helping people that you need to have in order to become a successful surgeon. "Do volunteer work at a hospital, get to know the docs, and then ask to do some job shadowing."

Patrick concludes that the most important motivation in his career is being able to "help people live better and enjoy their lives. I have many cards and photos," he says, "from anniversaries, vacations, and family events that my patients have been able to enjoy after their operations. It's very hard work, but I would do it all over again."

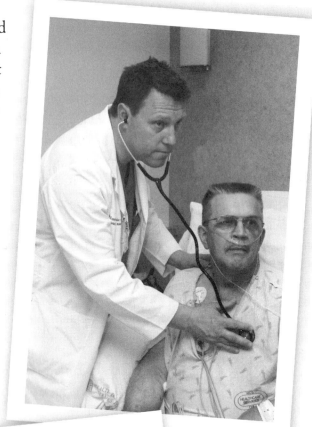

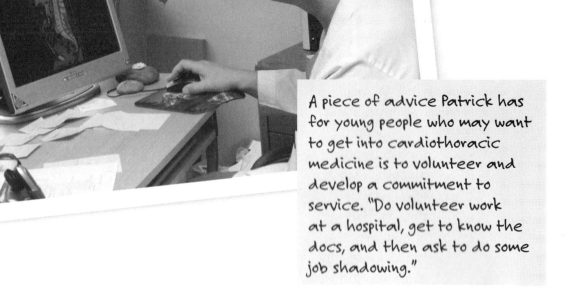

A piece of advice Patrick has for young people who may want to get into cardiothoracic medicine is to volunteer and develop a commitment to service. "Do volunteer work at a hospital, get to know the docs, and then ask to do some job shadowing."

Perfusionist
Pat Grady, Ohio

Heart and lung surgeries are difficult to perform and require a team of well-trained and focused people. When you think of surgeries like this, you probably think of the doctors and nurses who are working hard and long to ensure that the patient comes through the operation safely. Have you ever thought about *how* a patient stays alive while a surgeon works on his heart or on his lungs?

Pat Grady is one of the people at the Cleveland Clinic who make it possible for a cardiothoracic surgeon like Dr. Patrick Ryan to do his job. Pat is a perfusionist. His job is crucial to the success of an operation. He runs the heart and lung machine that breathes for a patient and pumps the patient's blood while he or she is being operated on. A person's life is truly in Pat's hands each time he goes to work.

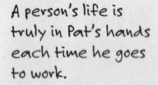

A person's life is truly in Pat's hands each time he goes to work.

"My main responsibility is to operate the heart-lung machine during open heart surgery," Pat says. "I take over the functions of the heart and lungs,

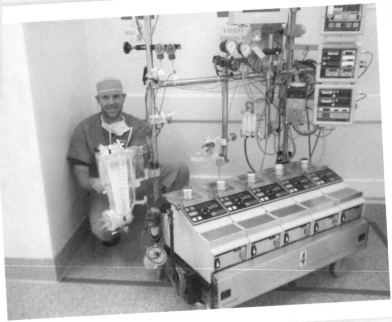

pump blood throughout the body, oxygenate and remove CO_2 from the blood, and provide a still and bloodless field so that the surgeon can operate."

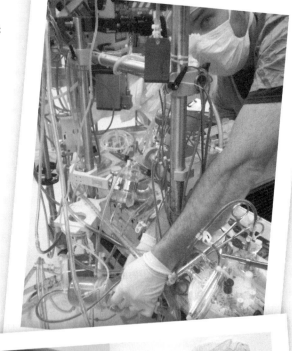

Pat knew that he wanted to work in the medical field when he entered college, but he didn't know exactly what job he would eventually take on. He had never heard of perfusion before he got to college. While there, he studied math and science, including calculus, anatomy and physiology, organic chemistry, and physics.

To be a successful perfusionist, you should have a desire to help others. "It is also important to be able to focus and make critical decisions quickly," Pat adds.

To become a perfusionist, you must become certified by the American Board of Cardiovascular Perfusion. This requires you to take two exams. One is a basic science exam, and the other is a clinical application test. Throughout your career, you must attend continuing education classes and workshops to stay on top of new and current developments in cardiothoracic surgery and perfusion technology.

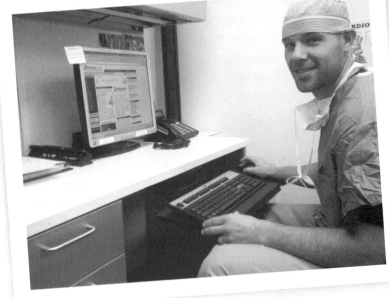

So, what does the future of perfusion technology hold? Who knows, but technology is constantly changing. For example, the Cleveland Clinic has begun to perform robotically assisted heart surgery. This is also called closed-chest heart surgery. Although the benefits to the patient are many, the task becomes infinitely more delicate for the surgical team.

Check out the Cleveland Clinic's website to learn more about robotically assisted heart surgery: http://my.clevelandclinic.org/heart/services/surgery/roboticallyassisted.aspx.

A surgeon uses a specially designed computer console to control robotic arms. There are tiny instruments on the ends of the arms that enter a patient's chest through a small incision.

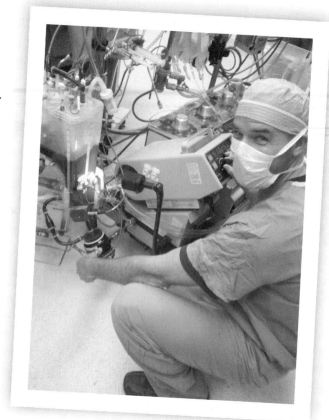

Because the incision is so small, a patient has a shorter recovery, less scarring, and less bleeding. There is a reduced chance for infection, and he or she can return to everyday tasks much more quickly. According to the Cleveland Clinic's website, "Robotically assisted heart surgery has changed the way certain heart operations are being performed. This technology allows cardiac surgeons to perform certain types of complex heart surgeries with smaller incisions and precise motion control, offering patients improved outcomes."

Although robotically assisted heart surgery is better for the patient, it presents new challenges for the perfusionist. Pat needs to insert the tubes that keep patients alive during surgery through smaller openings in different locations. He needs to thread them into the body from the groin area. When an open chest surgery is performed, Pat has open access to the organs he is taking over for. When the chest is closed, he, and perfusionists like him, need to find new ways to do their job.

Build a Robotic Arm

Robotics is changing the way we do things. From vacuum cleaners and lawn mowers that move themselves to surgeons performing complicated surgeries with the help of robotic arms like Pat talked about, technology has an effect on almost all we do. In this activity, you will use common materials to design a model of a robotic arm that can actually pick up a packing peanut. This is an open-ended activity. Use trial and error and your own creativity to design your robotic arm. If something doesn't work, try something else. If you discover another material that might work out, use it. The following materials list is really just a suggestion. Some of the greatest discoveries of our time have come about because someone was trying to design something else, or a person kept on trying— failure after failure. Look at any failed attempts you make critically. Why didn't your arm work? What could have been done differently? Then, try again.

Materials

- Styrofoam packing peanut
- Cardboard strips
- Binder clips
- Brads
- Craft sticks
- Yarn
- Metal hangers
- Florist's wire
- Pencils
- Paper clips
- String
- Foam scraps
- Fabric scraps

Procedure

1. Gather the materials on the list or other materials that you think might work.
2. Work alone or with a partner to sketch out an idea for a robotic arm that can pick up a packing peanut.
3. Build your arm and test it out.
4. Share your invention with someone. Then, try to improve your design so that it can pick up something even heavier.

Pat believes, "The coolest part of my job is seeing the heart start to beat again. During heart surgery, we need to stop the heart from beating; towards the end of the operation, it starts back up." The biggest surprise he has faced in his career is the autonomy, or independence, he faces on a daily basis. "When I am on call, I am the only one in the whole hospital that knows how to do this job. This brings with it a great responsibility because a patient's life is truly in my hands."

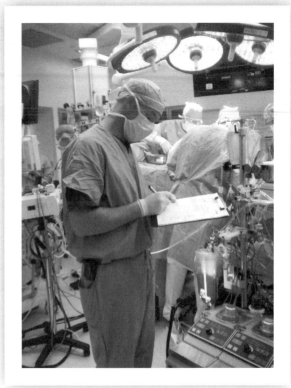

He concludes, "Perfusion is a challenging and rewarding career. Be curious, never stop learning and asking questions. If there is something that interests you, find out about it, and go observe someone doing that job."

"Be curious, never stop learning and asking questions. If there is something that interests you, find out about it, and go observe someone doing that job."

Developmental Biologist
Laura Dyer, North Carolina

> "Science is all around us, whether it is deciding how much baking soda to use in a cake or wondering why it is impossible to make certain basketball shots."

Laura Dyer, a postdoctoral associate at the University of North Carolina at Chapel Hill School of Medicine, loves the exploration aspect of science. And she knew from an early age that she wanted to be a part of it. "I did see myself as being a scientist, as early as middle school. The area of study changed—and continued to do so throughout college—but that basic desire to know more has helped me through." Now, she studies developmental biology. "I am particularly interested in how heart defects form. Ideally, I'd like to prevent them from happening in all humans!"

In college, Laura studied chemistry. She says that it gave her a great foundation for doing work at a lab bench, being careful when making solutions, and not being afraid of math. "Science is all around us," Laura says, "whether it is deciding how much baking soda to use in a cake or wondering why it is impossible to make certain basketball shots."

Let's Bake!

As Laura said, science is everywhere! Even in the kitchen when you bake a cake. Cakes bake because the heat of the oven causes a chemical reaction to occur between the ingredients in the batter. Each separate ingredient serves a purpose. The baking powder makes bubbles in the batter. This keeps your cake light and fluffy. Protein in eggs become hard when cooked, making your cake firm. Finally, the oil in the butter keeps your cake moist, so it doesn't dry out. What do you think will happen when you bake four cakes—a control, and three more, each leaving out a key ingredient?

Materials

- Four small cake or loaf pans
- Cooking spray
- Sugar
- Butter
- Eggs
- Vanilla extract
- Flour
- Baking powder
- Milk
- Cake knife
- Oven

Procedure

1. Prepare all four of your cake pans by spraying them with cooking spray.
2. Preheat your oven to 350 degrees.
3. Prepare your Control Cake.
   - Cream together ½ cup of sugar and ¼ cup of butter.
   - Add 1 egg.
   - Add 1 teaspoon of vanilla.
   - Combine ¾ cup of all-purpose flour with 1 teaspoon of baking powder.
   - Add the dry ingredients to the wet ingredients slowly, stirring as you add.
   - Stir in ¼ cup of milk until your batter is smooth.
   - Pour the batter into your cake pan and bake for 20–30 minutes, or until the top of the cake springs back from your touch.

4. Prepare Test Cake One (no butter).
   - Cream together ½ cup of sugar and 1 egg.
   - Add 1 teaspoon of vanilla.
   - Combine ¾ cup of all-purpose flour with 1 teaspoon of baking powder.
   - Add the dry ingredients to the wet ingredients slowly, stirring as you add.
   - Stir in ¼ cup of milk until your batter is smooth.
   - Pour the batter into your cake pan and bake for 20–30 minutes, or until the top of the cake springs back from your touch.

5. Prepare Test Cake Two (no baking powder).
   - Cream together ½ cup of sugar and ¼ cup of butter.
   - Add 1 egg.
   - Add 1 teaspoon of vanilla.
   - Add ¾ cup of all-purpose flour to the wet ingredients slowly, stirring as you add.
   - Stir in ¼ cup of milk until your batter is smooth.
   - Pour the batter into your cake pan and bake for 20–30 minutes, or until the top of the cake springs back from your touch.

6. Prepare Test Cake Three (no egg).
   - Cream together ½ cup of sugar and ¼ cup of butter.
   - Add 1 teaspoon of vanilla.
   - Combine ¾ cup of all-purpose flour with 1 teaspoon of baking powder.
   - Add the dry ingredients to the wet ingredients slowly, stirring as you add.
   - Stir in ¼ cup of milk until your batter is smooth.
   - Pour the batter into your cake pan and bake for 20–30 minutes, or until the top of the cake springs back from your touch.

7. Let all four cakes cool.
8. Cut a slice from each cake and study them side-by-side. Answer the following questions:
   - Do they look different? How?
   - Do they feel different? How?
   - Do they taste different? How?
   - What conclusion can you draw about the importance of adding the proper ingredients to the recipes you make?

Laura's day starts early. "I work with mice, and the earlier I get down to check on them, the sooner the rest of my day begins!" She works with DNA, trying to see if patients with specific heart defects have genetic defects in the genes she studies. Laura

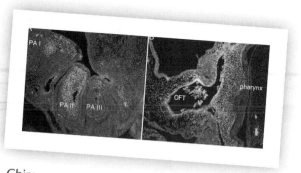

Chimeras created by grafting a quail and chick together.

also works with antibodies. "Each antibody is specific for a single protein, and certain proteins are present when a cell divides, or if the cell is dying." So, she can use the antibodies to determine if the cells are dividing or dying normally.

She says, "My absolute favorite thing is dissecting. In middle school, I was completely grossed out by the thought of cutting something open. Then, I took biology in high school, and we got to dissect fish, frogs, pigs, and the infamous shark, which smelled so bad that the entire school reeked during that week." Now, Laura dissects mice to find out what defects they have and how harmful they would be to a human baby because mice and humans are so similar.

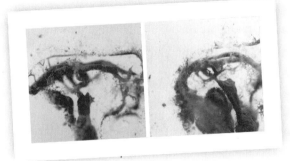

Ink-injected embryos.

Mouse Heart Discussion

Humans and mice are genetically similar. Really! According to *The New York Times*, an analysis of the mouse genome showed it to be remarkably similar to the human genome (Wade, 2002). And, because mice are small and relatively easy to care for, the genetic similarities make them ideal lab subjects. For example, if there is a genetic defect causing heart problems in humans, scientists can isolate the counterpart gene in a mouse and study it to see if there are ways to prevent this defect from occurring again in humans. They also can try to find treatment options for people suffering from genetic diseases. If you are interested in learning more about this interesting phenomenon, check out *The New York Times* article at: http://www.nytimes.com/2002/12/05/us/comparing-mouse-genes-to-man-s-and-finding-a-world-of-similarity.html?pagewanted=1.

A mouse heart and a human heart also are very similar. Compare the diagrams below. What are the similarities and differences? How can these similarities and differences between the anatomy of a mouse and human heart and the corresponding genetic material make mice good subjects for curing heart disease? How might scientists use this information to design laboratory tests? Either write a critical journal entry about this or enter into a critical discussion with classmates about the pros and cons of using live animals in science research, mice in particular.

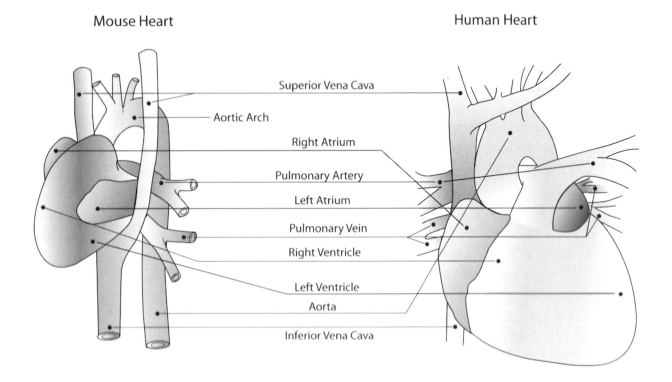

Mouse Heart   Human Heart

Superior Vena Cava

Aortic Arch

Right Atrium

Pulmonary Artery

Left Atrium

Pulmonary Vein

Right Ventricle

Left Ventricle

Aorta

Inferior Vena Cava

Laura admits that each of the huge "ta-dahs" of science that we hear about in the news are the result of years and years of research from across the globe, and are likely the product of many different people's work. She says, "I hope that my research can make an impact in the lives of babies with heart defects, lessening the severity or eliminating them altogether." She says that she now studies science because of some important mentors, including her mom, who is still a science teacher today, and her high school biology and chemistry teachers, who showed her that science is fun.

Laura admits that each of the huge "ta-dahs" of science that we hear about in the news are the result of years and years of research from across the globe, and are likely the product of many different people's work.

She concludes, "I spent 2 years volunteering in a fifth-grade classroom and one of my favorite activities was having students draw what a scientist looked like. Every picture was an old White man wearing a lab coat and glasses. The students were so confused to find out I was a scientist." She goes on, "There is no one picture of what a scientist looks like." A scientist can be a cheerleader—physics in motion. A scientist can be a band leader—music is rooted in mathematics, the language of science. A scientist can be a volunteer at an animal shelter—biology and psychology. There is science in everyone's life—you can be a scientist too!

Online Science Catalogs

The following websites offer science materials for purchase that may be useful as your students complete the activities in this book. Before you buy, check the prices of several sites to make sure that you are getting the right materials at the right price. I have purchased live cockroaches and other small animals from Carolina Biological Supply before and I love the large "baby soda bottle" test tubes offered at Steve Spangler's site. The other websites offer a wide range of supplies suitable for both classroom and home experimentation.

Science Kit and Boreal Laboratories
http://sciencekit.com

Carolina Biological Supply
http://www.carolina.com

WARD'S Natural Science
http://wardsci.com

Science Stuff
http://www.sciencestuff.com

Home Science Tools
http://www.hometrainingtools.com

The Nature Store
http://thenaturestore.com

Steve Spangler Science
http://www.stevespanglerscience.com

References

National Research Council. (1996). *National science education standards*. Washington, DC: National Academy Press.

Wade, N. (2002, December 5). Comparing mouse genes to man's and finding a world of similarity. *The New York Times*. Retrieved from http://www.nytimes.com

About the Author

Colleen Kessler is passionate about kids, learning, science, and books, and she indulges those passions every day as a science and education writer. Whether she is in her office overlooking her backyard, a National Wildlife Federation Certified Wildlife Habitat, taking a hike through the nearby meadows or woods, or trying out new experiments for her books with her three kids, Colleen engages in science all of the time.

"I love nature and all of its surprises," says Colleen. "Sitting by the small pond we have in the backyard in the springtime, and listening to the call of the amphibians, I know that there is nothing I'd rather be doing. How many people can work from home, doing a job they love, surrounded by their family, friends, and frogs?

"Just last night, my son and I took some flashlights, pulled on our rain boots and coats, and hiked out to a vernal pool at midnight. The world was silent outside the woods, but the deeper we walked, the louder the concert became. Spring peepers, wood frogs, and a green frog or two serenaded us as we balanced in the muck at the pool's downward slope. Around our feet swam the salamanders—Jefferson and Spotted—who had instinctively traveled, like so many before them, across the road to lay their eggs in the protected waters. Part research for a book on migration, part nature lesson, part bonding time with my son. I love my life!"

Colleen has written textbook chapters, teacher resources, lessons, experiments, games, leveled readers, and more for numerous educational publishers. She is the author of science books including *Hands-On Ecology*, *Super Smart Science*, *A Project Guide to Birds and Reptiles*, and *A Project Guide to the Solar System*. She can be reached at colleen@colleen-kessler.com. Check out Colleen's website: http://www.colleen-kessler.com.

Welcome

He's a singer, an actor, a fashion icon and one of the biggest stars in the world, but how well do you *really* know Harry Styles? If you're reading this, then we imagine the answer is pretty well, but inside you're sure to discover even more! And that's not all, you can also test your Harry knowledge with our fun and fiendish quiz questions and compare your results with friends to see who really knows Harry best!

Covering everything from Harry's school days and his first band to his *X Factor* adventure, his time in One Direction, his solo endeavours and his move into Hollywood, there's something for even the biggest Harry fans to learn and questions to test even the most hardcore Stylers!

In each article you'll find three questions with a range of difficulties – the harder the question, the more points it's worth (Bronze = 1, Silver = 2, Gold = 3) – and a maximum of six points available per article. You'll find some answers in the text, while others may require a little more brainpower and research skills!

So why not grab a notepad and pen and see how well you really know Harry, then compare scores with friends' to discover who's the ultimate Harry superfan!
Answers on page 122.
Enjoy!

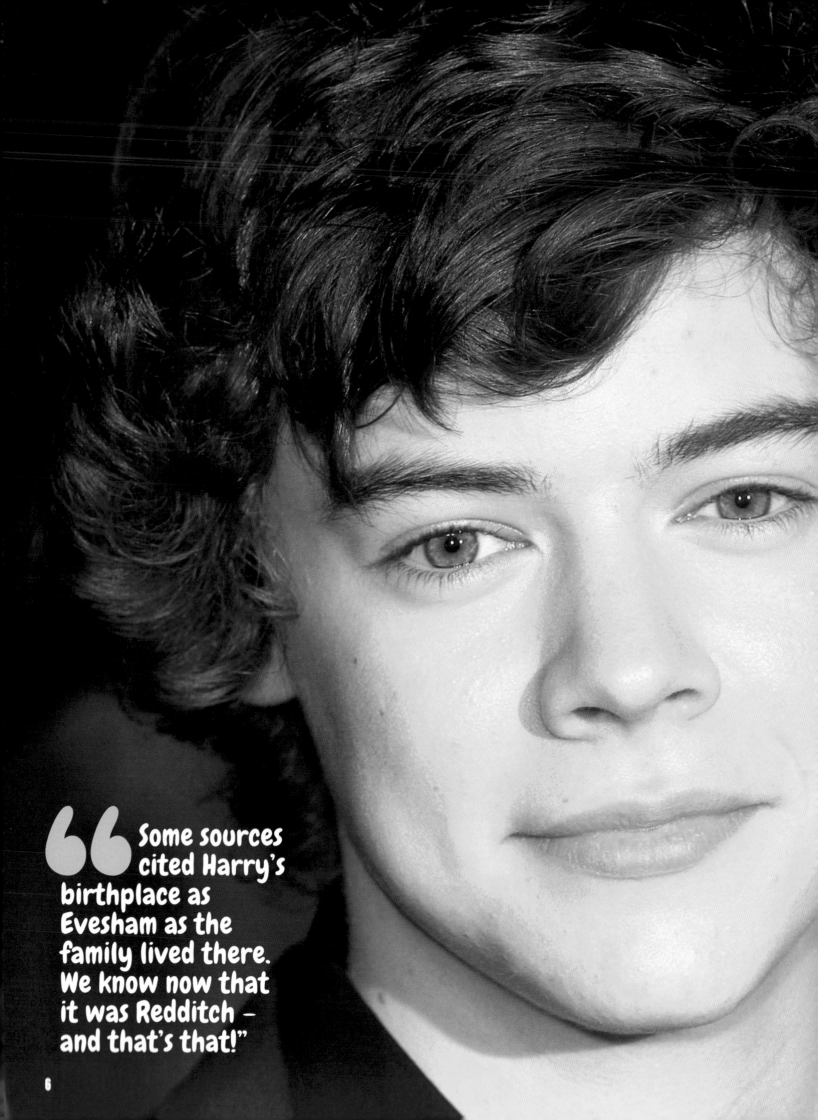

"Some sources cited Harry's birthplace as Evesham as the family lived there. We know now that it was Redditch – and that's that!"

Early life

A STAR IS BORN: THE MOMENT WHEN YOUNG HARRY FIRST CAME INTO THE WORLD

Harry Edward Styles was born on 1 February 1994 at the Alexandra Hospital in the town of Redditch in Worcestershire, although his birth was registered in the nearby town of Bromsgrove. This caused some confusion, which was only settled in later years when, in response to questions from Harry's fans, his father Des tweeted: 'He was born in Redditch, we were there just in time!'

This didn't quite solve the problem, though: some sources cited Harry's birthplace as Evesham, also in Worcestershire, because the family lived there when he was born, and also Holmes Chapel, in Cheshire, as they moved there a few years later. Still, we know now that it was Redditch – and that's that!

Meet Harry Styles: the hottest pop singer of his generation.

Des worked in finance, while Harry's mother Anne was a landlady. Harry also has an older sister, Gemma, about whom he once said, "She was always smarter than me, and I was always jealous of that." Harry described his upbringing in Cheshire as "quite boring, nothing much happens there… [but] it's quite picturesque," on his first appearance on *The X Factor* in September 2010. Still, he has always made it clear that he had a great childhood, with his parents introducing him to a variety of music at an early age.

As a toddler, Harry would listen to Des's collection of music by the Rolling Stones, Fleetwood Mac, Queen and Pink Floyd. Of the last of these, whose psychedelic *The Dark Side of the Moon* album was beloved in the Styles household, he remembered: "I couldn't really get it, but I just remember being like – this is really cool. Then my mom would always have Shania Twain, Savage Garden and Norah Jones going on."

It wasn't long before the young lad was singing songs himself, enabled by a karaoke machine that he was given by his grandfather. A favourite was Elvis Presley's 'The Girl of My Best Friend', he said.

"I had a really nice upbringing. I feel very lucky," he said. "I had a great family and always felt loved. There's nothing worse than an inauthentic tortured person. 'They took my allowance away, so I did heroin'. It's like – that's not how it works."

Still, a seismic change awaited Harry: at the age of seven, his parents sat him down and explained that Des would be moving out. Asked about that moment by Cameron Crowe in *Rolling Stone* magazine, Styles replied: "I don't remember. Honestly, when you're that young, you can kind of block it out… I mean, I was seven. It's one of those things. Feeling supported and loved by my parents never changed."

Harry remains close to both of his parents, fortunately. Anne later married her business partner John Cox, although that marriage also led to divorce: she tied the knot a third time to Robin Twist in 2013. Harry was her best man at the ceremony and, through Robin, gained an older stepbrother named Mike and a stepsister named Amy. Sadly, Robin died of cancer four years after the wedding, making Harry keen to take care of Anne after the upheavals she had been through.

"Since I've been 10," he said, "[I've wanted to] protect Mum at all costs… My mum is very strong. She has the greatest heart. [Her house in Cheshire] is where I want to go when I want to spend some time."

Harry and his older sister, Gemma, pictured in 2016.

Gemma, Harry and radio DJ Nick Grimshaw out on the town in 2013.

A scene from Holmes Chapel, Cheshire: "Nothing much happens there," said Harry.

> **He has always made it clear that he had a great childhood, with his parents introducing him to a variety of music at an early age"**

Test your Harry knowledge!

CAN YOU HIT THE GOLDEN NOTE?

 Q1: Where was Harry born?

 Q2: What's Harry's sister's name?

 Q3: Which Elvis song was one of Harry's favourites to sing on his karaoke machine?

Grab a notepad and pen and see how well you know Harry.

Answers on p122

School days

PAY ATTENTION, STYLES! WHAT WAS HARRY LIKE AS A CHEEKY SCHOOLBOY IN HOLMES CHAPEL?

As a four-year-old, Harry went to Hermitage Primary School in Holmes Chapel, where his first teacher, Mrs Vernon, did a great job of looking after him. We know this because when he played a massive show at the Old Trafford stadium in Manchester in June 2022, he stopped the show and said, "This is an absolute pleasure to be here at my home show, I cannot begin to tell you how much it means to me to play here tonight and all of you for coming. Some of the happiest times of my entire life have been making these last couple of albums, and some of the happiest times of my life have been right around the corner from here. So it feels pretty perfect to me playing these songs to you here tonight."

Poignantly, he told the crowd that his first teacher, Mrs Vernon, was in the crowd and asked

The guitar man, live in 2022.

Holmes Chapel Leisure Centre, next to Harry's school, where the young Styles no doubt played sports.

Manchester's Old Trafford stadium, packed with fans waiting for Harry.

where she was. After a moment, a surprised-looking woman popped up on the huge screens and Harry said, "How are you? I heard you're retiring. I just want to thank you for everything in those formative years. Thank you so much… It means a lot to me that you're here tonight, you were truly wonderful teachers [sic]. Thank you from the bottom of my heart, and it means a lot that you're here and I'm dedicating this next song to you."

He then chuckled, "Can you imagine dealing with me when I was four? I was very fun," before launching into 'Canyon Moon', the perfect song for the occasion as it contains the line 'I'm going, oh, I'm going home'.

Now, the fact that the woman on the screens was not Mrs Vernon, who wasn't even at the show, makes this story even more awesome. The real Mrs Vernon was tracked down the next day by the producers of the morning TV show *Lorraine*, on which she appeared for an interview. As she told Lorraine: "I would have loved to have been there but Mrs Bailey, my colleague who was there, she phoned straight away. I've watched the video and it was just such a lovely tribute and a really, really great thing for him to do."

Asked by Lorraine whether Harry was always a "wee angel" during his primary school days, his former teacher remarked: "Some of the time. Some of the time he was an angel. Some of the time he could be, you know…

he's got a cheeky, lovely side to him. He was a great character. That smile was always so lovely. He loved music, he loved performing, right the way through our school and everybody, every teacher at Hermitage had a big impact on him."

She added: "I think there was something special – a sparkle, a twinkle in his eye, his personality, [his] character being so much there from when he was four or five. That showed us that he was going to go on to do something really special. But I don't think anybody could foresee just how mega and crazy, so huge his career would become. It is just outstanding."

It sounds like Harry got an A+ on his report card for stopping the show. The kid has a bright future ahead of him!

A hopeful fan on the way into the Old Trafford stadium where Harry played in June 2022.

Test your Harry knowledge!

CAN YOU HIT THE GOLDEN NOTE?

Q1: What was Harry's primary school called?

Q2: What was the name of Harry's first teacher?

Q3: What line from 'Canyon Moon' suited the moment perfectly?

Grab a notepad and pen and see how well you know Harry.
Answers on p122

Images: Getty Images

First band

ROCK AND ROLL WAS CALLING...
BUT IT TOOK A WHILE FOR THE YOUNG
HARRY STYLES TO ANSWER!

Canadian singer Bryan Adams wrote the legendary 'Summer Of '69'
song, covered by Harry's band, White Eskimo.

Harry had been a singer in private since his childhood, later citing Freddie Mercury, Elvis Presley and The Beatles as his musical influences, but he'd never seriously considered joining a band. One day, though, when Harry and his friend Nick Clough were working at a bakery shop, a customer asked Nick as he was serving at the counter, who was singing out the back. It was Harry, who was warbling away to himself while sweeping up outside.

"Have you ever thought about singing professionally? If you ever consider it, give me a call," said the unnamed customer, and although Harry never got around to doing so, the spark had been ignited. He and Nick would jam at Harry's house, with Nick playing guitar while Harry sang along or played a tambourine, but neither boy was particularly confident about his musical abilities.

Things took a step up when a friend at Holmes Chapel Comprehensive, Will Sweeny, decided to put together a rock band at school. Nick would be the bass player, which was a slight disappointment to Harry as he wanted to play that instrument himself, while Will took on the drums and another friend called Haydn Morris would play the guitar.

At first, Harry was worried about being the singer, not only because he preferred the idea of bass – it was also because he genuinely thought

Just a year after the school battle of the bands, here's 16-year-old Harry.

Images: Getty Images

15

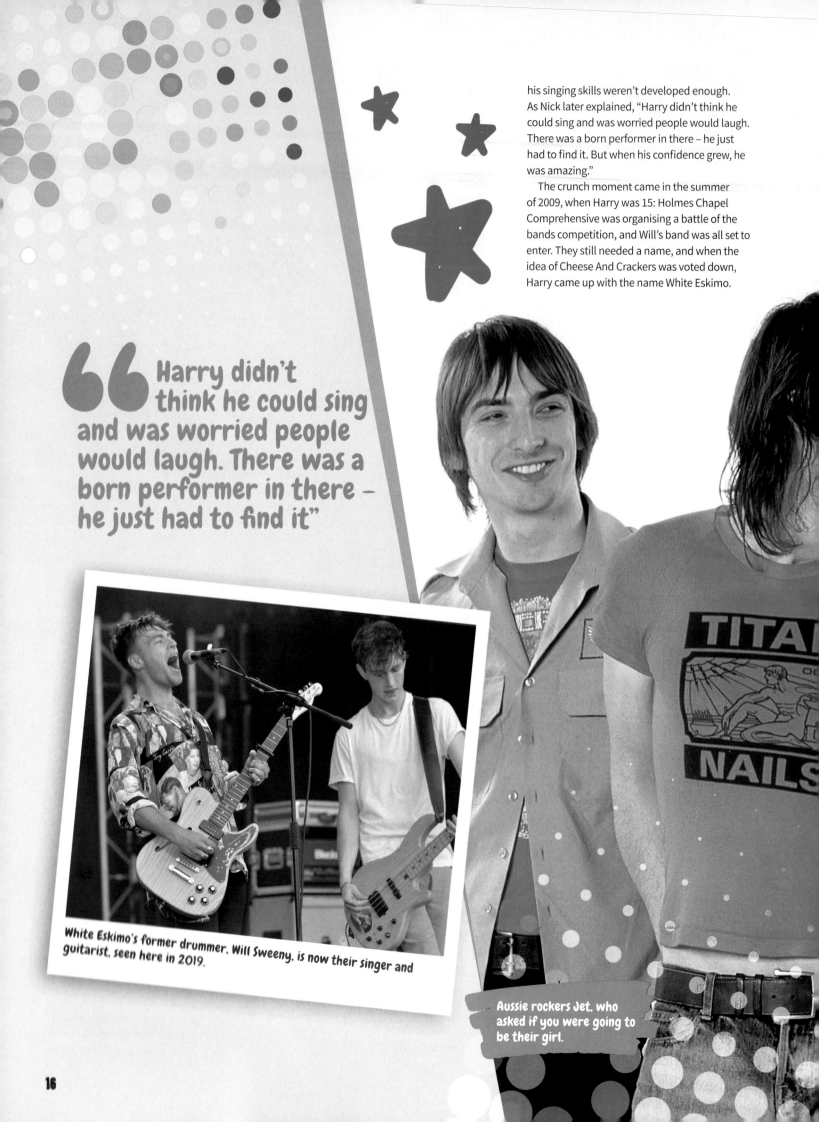

his singing skills weren't developed enough. As Nick later explained, "Harry didn't think he could sing and was worried people would laugh. There was a born performer in there – he just had to find it. But when his confidence grew, he was amazing."

The crunch moment came in the summer of 2009, when Harry was 15: Holmes Chapel Comprehensive was organising a battle of the bands competition, and Will's band was all set to enter. They still needed a name, and when the idea of Cheese And Crackers was voted down, Harry came up with the name White Eskimo.

> Harry didn't think he could sing and was worried people would laugh. There was a born performer in there – he just had to find it"

White Eskimo's former drummer, Will Sweeny, is now their singer and guitarist, seen here in 2019.

Aussie rockers Jet, who asked if you were going to be their girl.

Rehearsing for two weeks, the new band honed two songs – 'Summer Of '69' by Bryan Adams, and 'Are You Gonna Be My Girl' by Jet – and worked on their stage costumes. On the big day, Harry dressed in a white shirt and black tie and belted out the songs with more energy than confidence, but they pulled it off: White Eskimo won the day and walked off with £100 and the chance to play at a local festival called Goosfest in the nearby village of Goostrey.

History was made that day, and White Eskimo went on to perform more shows over the next year or so, with a setlist that included songs by Blink-182, Paolo Nutini, The Zutons and The Beatles. One time they were paid the princely sum of £400 to play at the wedding of the mother of one of the kids from school. They even tried writing songs of their own, one of which was called 'Gone In A Week'.

Inspired by the band's local popularity, Harry wondered what the next step would be if he wanted to further his musical career. Any ideas what his next move was?

Test your Harry knowledge!
CAN YOU HIT THE GOLDEN NOTE?

Q1: What name did the boys reject for their band?

Q2: Who wrote 'Are You Gonna Be My Girl'?

Q3: Are White Eskimo still going? (Google it!)

Grab a notepad and pen and see how well you know Harry.
Answers on p122

The X Factor Solo

HARRY'S FIRST BITE AT THE X FACTOR CHERRY – WAS IT ALWAYS DOOMED TO FAIL?

You can thank Harry's mother, Anne Twist, for making her son into a megastar – because it was her idea to get him to try out for *The X Factor*.

"I'd gone because my mum told me I was good from singing in the car," Harry later recalled, "but your mum tells you things to make you feel good, so you take it with a pinch of salt. I didn't really know what I was expecting when I went on there."

What Harry had was plenty of support from his mum Anne and stepfather Robin, who were at the first audition in Manchester on 11 April 2010, wearing shirts displaying his name. Will Sweeny was also there, the boys having taken a cheeky day off school to take their shot at stardom. Harry himself was dressed in a long, looped scarf and long cardigan, with curly locks that were quite different from the hair-gel waves and buzzcuts sported by many of the other hopefuls in the 'Boys' category.

Walking on stage in front of 3,000 fans plus Simon Cowell, Louis Walsh and Nicole Scherzinger would be enough to terrify even

> Slamming the door on *The X Factor*: Harry faces down his disappointment.

Dannii Minogue, Simon Cowell and Cheryl Cole in 2010: hard to impress.

When you're feeling down because a TV talent show said no, slip into your favourite onesie.

Test your Harry knowledge!

CAN YOU HIT THE GOLDEN NOTE?

Q1: What was Harry wearing in his first audition?

Q2: Who drove him to Wembley?

Q3: Which judge voted 'no' to Harry before Simon's vital vote?

Grab a notepad and pen and see how well you know Harry.
Answers on p122

the most experienced performer, but Harry looked nonchalant, having already appeared on camera beforehand when he told Dermot O'Leary, "I'm 16 and I'm from Holmes Chapel in Cheshire. It's a bit boring. Nothing much happens. It's picturesque." His first song, Train's 'Hey, Soul Sister', fell flat, but when Simon suggested that he try his second choice, Stevie Wonder's 'Isn't She Lovely', he did a fabulous job.

Nicole voted yes, saying, "You could really hear how great your voice was," but Louis thought Harry was too young and said, "It's a no from me." Fortunately, Simon gave the casting vote in Harry's favour, commenting, "You actually could be very good."

The next stage was the dreaded Bootcamp, at Wembley Arena in London. Harry's sister, Gemma, drove him down and left him chatting with the other contenders in the car park. When Simon appeared, he told everyone: "Today, you're going to be put into your categories and you're going to sing one song. There are literally no second chances today."

Asked to sing Michael Jackson's 'Man In The Mirror', Harry did a decent job, and had a few drinks with other contenders that night before an early start the next morning for the dancing round. Harry strutted his stuff with confidence – and it was time to see who had been voted through to the Judges' Houses stage.

It was getting serious at this point. With one more song to sing, would Harry make it?

Unbelievably from today's point of view, the answer was no. His name was not called, as he'd sung a version of Oasis's 'Stop Crying Your Heart Out', a tough song for a 16-year-old boy to sing. He admitted that his performance had been "boring" – and went home, his dreams in tatters.

Images: Getty Images

"You're too young, Harry!" said the X Factor judge Louis Walsh, perhaps unreasonably.

The X Factor
One Direction

GOING SOLO DIDN'T WORK OUT FOR HARRY THE FIRST TIME... BUT HIS BAND WAS A TRIUMPH!

Harry wasn't disappointed for long – because a phone call soon came from the production team at *The X Factor*, asking him if he'd like to return and compete in the 'Bands' category. Simon Cowell had been impressed with Harry and four other competitors in the 'Boys' category – Niall Horan, Liam Payne, Louis Tomlinson and Zayn Malik (like you don't know that already!) – and arranged for all five to form a new group.

The new band gelled immediately. "The minute they stood there for the first time together – it was a weird feeling," said Cowell in *Rolling Stone*. "They just looked like a group

at that point. I had a good feeling, but then obviously we had about a five-week wait where they had to work together. They had to come back for another section of the show where they performed together as a group for the first time. I was concerned whether five weeks was long enough, but they came back five weeks later and were absolutely sensational."

Harry suggested the name 'One Direction' to his new bandmates, who agreed to use it, and the game was on. Their first major challenge was the Judges' Houses stage, in their case the home of Cowell in Spain. Having failed and come back, One Direction had an air of the underdog

The brand-new One Direction, with their mentor Simon Cowell, take their first steps into history.

about them, which gave them immense public support – so when they easily passed the Judges' Houses stage, there was a huge swell of excitement among viewers of the show.

"When they came to my house in Spain and performed," remembered Cowell, "I tried to keep a straight face for a bit of drama for the show. I remember sitting next to this girl who I was working with. The second they left we jumped out of my chair and said, 'These guys are incredible!' They just had it. They had this confidence. They were fun. They worked out the arrangements themselves. They were like a gang of friends, and kind of fearless as well."

Remember, kids, staying hydrated is important: Harry steps out in 2010.

Images: Getty Images

23

WOLVERHAMPTON
IS GOING IN
ONE
DIRECTION
UP
⬆ ⬆

Wolverhampton council's design budget may not have been huge – but it's the thought that counts!

The veteran talent-spotter was right: One Direction were friends from the start. Fans and viewers spotted this instantly, and the social media networks lit up with 1D posts. That might seem obvious nowadays, but in 2010 – when *The X Factor* hit its peak viewership – the influence of Facebook and Twitter was new. One Direction were the first major pop band of the social media age, and as such, their rise was historic. Instagram was only launched the same year, but blew up quickly, with 1D posts soon seen there too. The world – and its phone – was on One Direction's side.

This meant that actually, it didn't matter if Harry and the boys won *The X Factor* or not – and ultimately they didn't, coming in third after Matt Cardle and Rebecca Ferguson. They immediately signed a record deal with Cowell's label, Syco Music, and took their first steps into history. The world lay at their feet, and we were there to see it happen.

Test your Harry knowledge!
CAN YOU HIT THE GOLDEN NOTE?

🎵 **Q1:** Name the other four members of One Direction

🎵 **Q2:** Who came first and second in *The X Factor* in 2010?

🎵 **Q3:** Which X Factor judge was 1D's mentor?

Grab a notepad and pen and see how well you know Harry.
Answers on p122

When 1D arrived for a show in Wolverhampton, the crowds went wild.

25

The birth Of 1D

BETWEEN THE X FACTOR AND THEIR DEBUT ALBUM, ONE DIRECTION HAD A LOT ON THEIR TO-DO LIST...

The record business uses the word 'business' for a reason; when there's money to be made and vast fortunes on the table, everybody involved becomes very businesslike. In the case of One Direction, this applied even to Simon Cowell, who said of their deal with Syco: "I thought, 'As long as we can get the right record, they've got a great shot'. This was such an important signing, we let three or four of the Sony labels make a presentation. I didn't automatically give it to my own label. I thought, 'This is so important, if somebody can come up with a better idea...' I was actually

"The next job was to promote the new band and get deals signed for the rest of the world"

26

The face of a new generation: Harry is deep in thought as 2011 rolls around.

Harry tries not to laugh mid-song as One Direction wow the crowd.

willing to pass them along to another division of Sony because I thought the group were that important. I thought they were going to be so massive, I was prepared to do that."

It turned out that Syco was the right home for the new band, in the UK at least, so the next job was to promote the new band and get deals signed for the rest of the world. With that in mind, One Direction starred at the Pride of Britain Awards at the Grosvenor House hotel in London's Park Lane, and showed up on the red carpet at the premiere of *Harry Potter and the Deathly Hallows: Part 1* at the Odeon in Leicester Square.

On Capital FM in winter 2011 – hot on the promotional trail for album number one.

After Harry enjoyed a quiet Christmas at home with his family and friends back in Cheshire, he was off to Los Angeles, staying at the W Hotel in West Beverly Hills. He and Louis enjoyed a shopping trip in Rodeo Drive before being introduced to the producers who would write songs and record the band in sessions for their forthcoming studio album. Meetings took place with the Swedish pop producers RedOne, Carl Falk and Rami Yacoub, who had worked on 'Baby One More Time' and 'Oops! I Did it Again' for Britney Spears, as well as songs for Backstreet Boys and Westlife.

Before they could head to Sweden to record the album, One Direction had shows to play – on the annual X Factor Live Tour, which kicked off in February 2011 at Birmingham's LG Arena. They were asked to perform five songs: Rihanna's 'Only Girl (In The World)', 'Chasing Cars' by Snow Patrol, 'Kids In America' by Kim Wilde, Kelly Clarkson's 'My Life Would Suck Without You', and 'Forever Young', the winner's song that they would have performed in the TV final.

Moving into a luxury apartment in the suburb of Barnet, just north of London, Harry and Louis settled in to the lifestyles of the young pop star, with all the media attention that comes with it. Fortunately, their flat was hidden from the intrusive photo-lenses of the paparazzi.

After the X Factor Live Tour finished in April, Harry, Louis and friends took a week off to go skiing in Courchevel in the French Alps. A novice at the sport, Harry needed some help. Fortunately, he didn't break any bones – that might have got in the way of his very first recording sessions, which lay just around the corner.

Test your Harry knowledge!

CAN YOU HIT THE GOLDEN NOTE?

Q1: Which *Harry Potter* film premiere did 1D appear at?

Q2: Which bandmate did Harry share an apartment with?

Q3: Can you name all five songs that 1D played on the X Factor Live Tour?

Grab a notepad and pen and see how well you know Harry.
Answers on p122

"They were the first British group to have their debut album reach Number One in the United States"

Up All Night

WHEN 1D FINALLY UNLEASHED THEIR DEBUT ALBUM, IT MADE AN IMPACT ALL AROUND THE WORLD

Harry knew that One Direction had struck gold with their first album – *Up All Night*, an apt title given his band's leisure and work schedules – when he heard the song 'What Makes You Beautiful'. Written by Savan Kotecha, the song impressed Harry so much that he sent Savan a text reading simply, 'I think you got it. I think you got the one here'. Savan, delighted with this, kept the text.

If there was any doubt that One Direction had a bright future ahead of them, it was dispelled permanently when *Up All Night* made them the first British group to have their debut album reach Number One in the United States. Think about what that means: The Beatles didn't do that, The Rolling Stones didn't do that, Led Zeppelin, Duran Duran, the Spice Girls and Take That didn't do that.

On the album, on which Harry has three co-writing credits, you can hear that his slightly raspy voice stands out a little from the clean tones of the other four. That's an advantage, as he has his own sound and was able to handle music of a more rock-indebted nature later in his career. The album as a whole has a guitar edge that helps it to avoid sounding like yet another smooth boy-band record, and fans appreciated this, with guitar

Stairway to heaven: One Direction in 2011, ready for an album signing.

31

Lean on me: Liam and Harry at Amazon's warehouse in Ridgmont, England.

Ed Sheeran in 2011: on the cusp of worldwide success. A year before, he wrote 'Moments' for 1D.

Test your Harry knowledge!

CAN YOU HIT THE GOLDEN NOTE?

Q1: Who wrote 'What Makes You Beautiful'?

Q2: Which New York venue did 1D play?

Q3: How many copies has *Up All Night* sold worldwide?

Grab a notepad and pen and see how well you know Harry.
Answers on p122

The famous Radio City Music Hall in New York, where 1D played in 2011.

covers of 'What Makes You Beautiful' found all over YouTube.

One of the album's best songs didn't actually make it onto the regular edition. This was 'Moments', which appeared on the deluxe version of *Up All Night* and which was written by none other than Ed Sheeran, himself a year or so away from massive fame. Harry knew Ed, the two having been introduced by a guitarist, Chris Leonard, and asked him to deliver a song or two for consideration. The song they chose, 'Moments', is a heartbreaker, with the prominent line, "If I could only have this life for one more day."

The next move for One Direction was to sign a deal in America with Columbia Records, who were experiencing the rapid rise of their star act, Adele, at the time. Columbia thought that there was a gap in the music industry in the USA for a boy band, now that the Nineties' stars Backstreet Boys and NSYNC were long gone – even though non-American boy bands tend not to do particularly well there. The deal was signed, and now One Direction had an American home.

The Americans knew what they were doing, tapping into the rising social media wave of support for their new band and making sure that wherever you went online that year, you saw One Direction's name. The label reacted quickly to the success of 'What Makes You Beautiful', bringing the American release of *Up All Night* forward by a week to capitalise on it. A one-off show at Radio City in New York with the American boy band Big Time Rush, also signed to Columbia, was an early milestone in One Direction's career.

After *Up All Night*'s success, what was 1D's next move? Record a second album – fast.

> " One of the album's best songs didn't make it onto the regular edition. This was 'Moments', which appeared on the deluxe version of Up All Night and which was written by Ed Sheeran"

Images: Getty Images, Peter Whatley

33

Harry before performing on the American *X Factor* in 2012: is that a touch of lippy?

Take Me Home

WITH TWO ALBUMS OUT IN SUCH QUICK SUCCESSION, COULD 1D MAINTAIN THEIR MOMENTUM?

With a heavy travel schedule ahead of One Direction, *Take Me Home* was the perfect title for their second album, which came out in time for Christmas 2012. The boys were still excited about their newfound good fortune and enjoying their lifestyles, but the life of a pop band is a tough one, so the fact that some of the new songs were a little melancholy was no surprise.

Not that any of this affected the production or the commercial performance of the new record.

With an established sound based on upbeat pop with guitar elements, *Take Me Home* continued the mission that had begun with *Up All Night*. Recorded in Stockholm once again, with Savan Kotecha, Carl Falk and Rami Yacoub at the helm, the album was populated with songs that were infectious, catchy and designed for commercial appeal. The singers were all given writing credits, and an invitation was put out by Simon Cowell for songwriters who wished to contribute to the album.

Four of the 1D guys look happy, one does not. A glimpse of the future, perhaps?

Hitting the high notes on *The X Factor*, mere yards away from an adoring crowd.

Ed Sheeran submitted another song, this time one that he had worked on with a singer-songwriter called Fiona Bevan. The lyrics of the song 'Little Things', were inspired by the late author Virginia Woolf, about whom Ed explained: "She always looked at the minutiae and emotion of a situation. I'd been thinking about that a lot, and how the little things really represent the big things." Fiona added, "We were thinking of real people we loved, and the strange quirks and imperfections that made us love them. So everything in the song is real, which is a lovely thing to be able to say." It's one of the sweetest songs on *Take Me Home*, and an enduring fan favourite.

Heading out on tour to promote the new album, One Direction criss-crossed the globe, running into the great and the good of showbiz and politics along the way. One of the latter was America's First Lady, Michelle Obama, who had a long chat with all of the band: Harry reportedly asked her if she and President Barack Obama had trouble getting pizza delivered to the White House. Well, we've all pondered that question…

After America, it was time to head Down Under, and Harry wasted no time in getting to know the locals, cheering at wet T-shirt competitions and getting up close and personal with a model called Emma Ostilly. The tabloids went Styles crazy, having already had a field day with his earlier relationship with the TV presenter Caroline Flack – who you can read about elsewhere in this publication.

After this stage in One Direction's career had been successfully completed, it was all about keeping momentum rolling – and so it was decided that more recordings would be made, both audio and video. A third album was planned for release as soon as possible, with more mega-tours on the books. Would the circus go on forever? It certainly looked and felt that way from the outside.

The truth, of course, is never what it seems.

Test your Harry knowledge!

CAN YOU HIT THE GOLDEN NOTE?

Q1: Who inspired the song 'Little Things'?

Q2: Which model did Harry meet in Australia?

Q3: In which city did One Direction perform the first show of their Take Me Home tour?

Grab a notepad and pen and see how well you know Harry.
Answers on p122

"The tabloids went Styles crazy, having already had a field day with his earlier relationship with the TV presenter Caroline Flack"

Michelle and Barack Obama: no need to order pizza, they're clearly on their way out on the town.

Looking serious in Spain: One Direction were growing up fast, with the happy smiles less prevalent than before.

With *Midnight Memories*, 1D became the first band in US history to have their first three albums debut at Number One.

Midnight Memories

THREE'S A CHARM! ONE DIRECTION HIT PEAK FORM WITH MIDNIGHT MEMORIES...

What's a boy band to do when their booking agent has lined up shows around the world, but their record company wants new music? There's only one thing for it – get the new songs recorded on the road.

This is not as easy as it sounds. The Take Me Home tour of early 2013 may have involved long flights and endless waiting around to soundcheck, but that doesn't mean the 1D boys were in the mood for making new music. On the contrary, they were probably exhausted – but like the troopers they are, they knuckled down and got it done.

On the way, they would flip hotel-room beds up against the wall so that the rooms could function as makeshift recording studios, grabbing a few minutes before their next departure to the show or the airport to get some vocals down on portable hard drive.

Images: Getty Images

Test your Harry knowledge!

CAN YOU HIT THE GOLDEN NOTE?

Q1: Which two LA writers worked on *Midnight Memories*?

Q2: Whose scarlet album is mentioned?

Q3: How many copies did *Midnight Memories* sell in 2013?

Grab a notepad and pen and see how well you know Harry.
Answers on p122

Even after the show, when the singers were still on a high from performance adrenaline, they would take the opportunity to record some vocals: in some ways this benefited the final recordings, as they were packed full of energy and the boys' voices were fully warmed up.

This time around, two Los Angeles-based writers and producers, Julian Bunetta and John Ryan, took control of the sound of the album. Their idea was to give One Direction a more mature sound on the *Midnight Memories* album without sacrificing any of the elements that their fans loved: as Julian explained, "They needed to grow up or they were going to go away – and they wanted to grow up."

This time, Harry only had four co-writing credits – compare that to Louis' nine – but it was interesting to note that on the songs 'Happily' and 'Something Great', he was the only singer. Did this mean that he was starting to break away a little, creatively speaking? Maybe… just maybe.

Other songs on the record showcased some serious talent. Snow Patrol singer Gary Lightbody co-wrote the song 'Something Great' along with his band's producer Jacknife Lee. There was a further link to two other 1D friends – Ed Sheeran, who had toured with Snow Patrol in 2012, and Taylor Swift, on whose 2012 album *Red* the two musicians had worked. Taylor comes into this story a little later, as we will see.

Two singles set the scene for the new record, continuing the flow of 1D product that had been released since *The X Factor*, now three years in the rear-view mirror. 'Best Song Ever' and 'Story Of My Life' both featured Harry at front and centre, and their videos, directed by his friend – and at the time, also his landlord – Ben Winston, devoted a lot of screen time to him. Of the two clips, make sure you watch 'Story Of My Life' if you're a real Styles fan: it's made up of old family album photos, and the shots of Harry as a kid are endearing. His mum Anne features in the video too, making it a moment to cherish.

Blowing kisses to his public, Harry rocked a more mature look in 2013. What, no baggy jeans and hi-tops?

Four

WAS FOUR, THE ALBUM TITLE, A FORESHADOWING OF THE NEW 1D LINE-UP IN DUE COURSE?

There was little respite for One Direction in 2014. A new album was on the way for the fourth year in a row, with the expected mega-tour of stadiums accompanying it, and on top of that the band would be filming a live documentary called *Where We Are: The Concert Film*. The clear requirement was that Harry and his comrades would look and sound on top form: given the relatively short shelf-life of any pop band, a drop in professional standards signals the end of the road sooner rather than later. No pressure, then…

The documentary was filmed at the end of June at the San Siro Stadium in Milan. The director, Paul Dugdale, knew what he was doing, having previously worked with heavyweights such as Adele, Coldplay and The Prodigy. Harry's friend, Ben Winston was also involved as an executive producer. When *Where We Are* was shown in cinemas in the October of 2014, it did great business, taking an estimated $15 million worldwide and becoming the biggest ever 'event cinema movie', as its specific category was defined.

While the film's commercial performance was not disputed, the critics took a mixed view. One writer, *The Guardian*'s Leslie Felperin, wrote that Harry looked more handsome at the ripe old age of 21 than he had a few years earlier, but also added: "he also looks like he can barely conceal

Scooping yet another award in 2014: can a band have too much of a good thing?

The boy becomes a man: Harry faces up to his future in 2014.

Images: Getty Images

his boredom. He's literally just going through the motions." She also wrote that it was surely only a matter of time before he went off to make his first solo album.

You couldn't really blame Harry for being a little jaded. Anyone would find One Direction's conveyor-belt existence exhausting, and the constant pressure of obeying orders laid down from above would have been endlessly irritating. Who wouldn't dream of taking a break in that situation – and after that break, doing something more fulfilling on one's own terms?

Still, *Four* had to be recorded, and connecting once again with Julian Bunetta and John Ryan, One Direction did their duty. Harry's most notable contribution was on the song 'Stockholm Syndrome', a term that refers to the psychological attachment that prisoners can feel towards their captors. His lyrics weren't exactly sophisticated, with a chorus of, 'Oh baby, look what you've done to me', but come on, this music is supposed to be fun, first and foremost.

Once again, the album topped the charts in the UK and USA, making 1D the first band to have their first four albums debut at Number One in America – so their fanbase was obviously still enthusiastic. The critics were reasonably keen on it, too, with *Rolling Stone* stating that One Direction had 'mastered the ancient boyband art of whispering directly into listeners' ears', which might sound a touch creepy but was not intended that way. *Time* magazine pointed to the boys' 'maturation into men', and highlighted the 'spunky Styles-penned 'Stockholm Syndrome'.

Four years into their careers, 1D were still on top of the world, then. Their new music and their new movie had both reinforced their unprecedented levels of commercial success – but how long would it be before one of them had had enough?

Test your Harry knowledge!

CAN YOU HIT THE GOLDEN NOTE?

Q1: Who directed *Where We Are*?

Q2: How much money did *Where We Are* take at the box office?

Q3: Where did *Four* rank on Billboard's 200 Greatest Albums of the 2010s?

Grab a notepad and pen and see how well you know Harry.
Answers on p122

Are the smiles beginning to wear thin? Questions were asked in 2014.

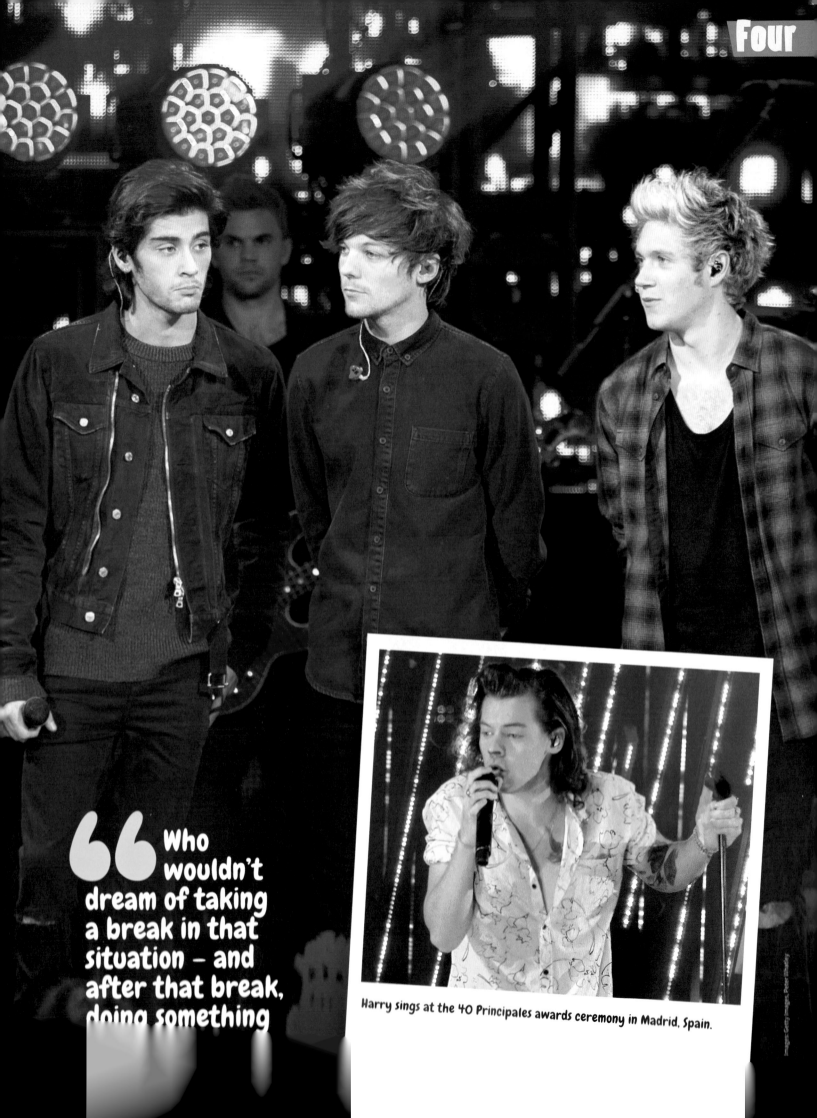

> **Who wouldn't dream of taking a break in that situation – and after that break, doing something**

Harry sings at the 40 Principales awards ceremony in Madrid, Spain.

Made In The A.M.

RECORDED IN CHAOS, COULD MADE IN THE A.M. BRING IT BACK FOR ONE DIRECTION?

When Zayn Malik announced on 25 March 2015 that he was quitting One Direction, the writing was effectively on the wall for the band. At first, Zayn was positive about the move and supportive of his former bandmates, but he soon changed his tune, firstly being neutral about them and then turning a little spiteful.

The timing of his departure was either unfortunate or beneficial, depending on your point of view: you could argue that it got people talking about One Direction just in time for their next album, *Made In The A.M.*, or you could equally reasonably state that Zayn's absence weakened the group, whose image had always been about friendship against the odds.

Harry pictured on a walkabout in London. Looking sharp, H!

See you later: Zayn Malik left One Direction in the spring of 2015.

Either way, *Made In The A.M.* received a lot of attention when it was released later that year. The remaining four singers had actually had a chance to think their situation over during its recording, as Harry explained when the record came out. "It was just the coolest time to sit and think," he reflected. "It gave us the chance to focus on writing good songs that we like and we wanted to listen to."

In his particular case, a song of his called 'If I Could Fly' became popular among Directioners, and continues to be a favourite when he plays it as a solo artist. Although his fans often asked who it was he was missing in the song's lyrics, he never told them. Instead, he explained accurately that love songs can be about several different people rather than just one. "They can be about a time or a place and you kind of personify it and stick a name on it, and then everyone thinks it's about a certain person, but I don't think it's always so black and white," he mused.

While two other Harry songs, 'Perfect' and 'Olivia', also attracted questions about their subject, he again chose to remain secretive. The latter was released as the new album's second single, after 'Drag Me Down', and came with a perfect video from the fans' point of view. Directed by the acclaimed director Sophie Muller, the black-and-white clip was shot at the

> ❝ **It gave us the chance to focus on writing good songs that we like and we wanted to listen to**❞

Images: Getty Images, Peter Whatley

Test your Harry knowledge!

CAN YOU HIT THE GOLDEN NOTE?

Q1: What date did Zayn announce his departure?

Q2: Who directed the 'Perfect' video?

Q3: What was the album's apt third and final single called?

Grab a notepad and pen and see how well you know Harry.
Answers on p122

InterContinental Hotel in New York, and showed the group having fun, playing golf, kicking a football, admiring the scenery, running down the hotel corridors or just lazing around.

The critics gave *Made In The A.M.* a mixed reception as per usual, with *NME* concluding that it was 'pretty silly' and adding, 'Now they can get on with the fall-outs, drug binges, bankruptcy and podginess'. *Rolling Stone* was kinder, saying that it was 'the kind of record the world's biggest pop group makes when it's time to say thanks for the memories'.

Harry stayed positive despite the varying response, describing the new album as, "the best album we feel we've done." It's a shame, then, that it was the first One Direction album not to enter the American charts at the top spot, beaten by Justin Bieber's *Purpose*. Still, it sold more than 2.4 million copies in the UK alone, making it a success by anyone's standards.

Perhaps the most telling comment came from Patrick Ryan, the primary writer of 'Perfect': although *USA Today* called it an 'exemplary pop song', he stated: "It's tough to promote a new album when everyone's marked your gravestone."

Not bothered: the new four-man 1D line-up were still having fun in 2015.

Enjoy those lovely locks while you can, Harry - they're coming off soon!

The end of 1D

AND SO IT ALL FELL APART... LEAVING HARRY FREE TO TAKE THE NEXT STEP FORWARD. GO, HARRY, GO!

When Simon Cowell was asked by *Rolling Stone* what the best way was to ensure the longevity of a band, he told them: "Be sensible and treat them as human beings, genuinely. That's the most important thing. Traditionally, record companies would put out the most possible product in a short period of time, thinking you only have two or three years. I don't think that's necessarily the case now. If you're sensible and you don't burn them out, you don't have to put a time limit on this any more. And they're so young, these guys."

"I told you not to wear that shirt!" On-stage bantz between Harry and Niall.

Harry is unsmiling and looking deep in thought.

Test your Harry knowledge!

CAN YOU HIT THE GOLDEN NOTE?

Q1: Why did Zayn say he was leaving 1D?

Q2: When did 1D announce their hiatus?

Q3: In which city was 1D's last ever concert?

Grab a notepad and pen and see how well you know Harry.
Answers on p122

How does that ethos square with the One Direction story? Well, they did last five years before calling it a day, in fairness: that's a long time in the fickle world of teenage pop, because something better is always around the corner. The members of 1D and the people who handled them got five albums, a couple of films and many, many stadium-sized live shows done before Zayn Malik quit and the band folded nine months later. No one got addicted to drugs, no one got depressed, no one went to jail – as far as we know – and a lot of people made a lot of money. The band also launched the solo career of our man Harry, too. All in all, then, the performance of One Direction as a creative and commercial entity could have been much, much worse.

Not that the split was fun for anyone at the time. In the official statement put out by the band on Facebook, Zayn said, "I want to be a normal 22-year-old who is able to relax and have some private time out of the spotlight. I know I have four friends for life in Louis, Liam, Harry and Niall. I know they will continue to be the best band in the world." Shortly afterwards, he told *Fader* magazine that One Direction's music was as "generic as f***" and added later that he "never really spoke to Harry" and that he had never been under the impression that they would keep in touch. Harry took the high road and never indulged in any trash talk towards Zayn, although he did humorously quip on *Saturday Night Live* in 2019: "I love those guys, they're my brothers: Niall, Liam, Louis and, uh, Ringo."

Generally, though, Harry stayed classy. When it was explained to him that Zayn had said, "[One Direction is] not music that I would listen to. If I was sat at a dinner date with a girl, I would play some cool shit, you know what I mean? I want to make music that I think is cool shit. I don't think that's too much to ask for," Harry replied: "I think it's a shame he felt that way, but I never wish anything but luck to anyone doing what they love. If you're not enjoying something and need to do something else, you absolutely should do that. I'm glad he's doing what he likes, and good luck to him."

When 1D announced in August 2015 that they would be taking a hiatus from the following March, the fanbase were saddened but not really surprised. Final dates in October left them knowing that the band appreciated them – and that this was far from the end.

For Harry, of course, it was just the beginning. "I love the band, and would never rule out anything in the future," he said. "The band changed my life, gave me everything."

Winding up 2015 with a bang: 1D take their leave.

Rocking out in 2015: Harry reaches for the stars, and the high notes.

> **Harry needed a break, so the Caribbean also functioned as a place to relax and recharge as well as a songwriting hangout"**

Suits you, sir: looking smouldering on stage in Sydney, Australia.

Going solo

OUT OF THE BAND AND INTO THE SOLO LIMELIGHT – IT WAS TIME TO HIT THE STUDIO!

Most artists retreat to their bedrooms to write songs, but Harry Styles isn't most artists, and when the time came to write songs for his debut solo album, he took off to Jamaica. In fairness to him, after the split from One Direction in 2015 and the exhausting filming of *Dunkirk* the following year – which you can read about in our next chapter – he needed a break, so the Caribbean also functioned as a place to relax and recharge as well as a songwriting hangout.

Harry had already secured a manager in the form of Jeffrey Azoff's Full Stop Management, as well as landing in the books of the talent agency CAA and scoring a record deal with Columbia Records, and as if that wasn't enough for a 23-year-old pop star, he'd also founded his own label, Erskine Records. Now he just needed to assemble Team Styles – the musicians, writers and producers who would accompany him on his solo journey.

His first choice was the Grammy Award-winning producer Jeff Bhasker, who is renowned for his work with Kanye West as musical director, and then on 'We Are Young' and 'Uptown Funk' by Mark Ronson. The two were cautious when they first met, with Bhasker asking to meet Harry for a preliminary interview. When Bhasker's dog walked over to Harry and licked his hand, Jeff later explained

Don't stop him now: Harry arriving in Japan for live solo dates.

that he thought, "This guy has something special."
When Harry then played him some White Stripes
songs as an indicator of where he wanted his new
music to go, the producer was even more impressed.

Harry also paired up with a guitar player, Mitch
Rowland, after being introduced by Mitch's room-
mate, a studio engineer called Ryan Nasci. Mitch,
who specialised in playing Seventies-style guitar riffs,
instantly hit it off with Harry, even though he'd never
seen the inside of a recording studio before. Bhasker
later said, "Mitch comes down, and the second he
plugged in his guitar and started playing, Harry's eyes
just lit up and he was like, 'This is the guy'." The story
famously goes that when Mitch told Harry that he
couldn't make a particular rehearsal because he had a
shift to do at a local pizza restaurant, Harry told him,
"Well, you might not need to do that any more."

Harry had become a musician of no mean skill
over the years, taking his craft seriously, although
he rarely needed to pick up an instrument when he
was recording or performing with One Direction.
Things had changed now, and his happy memories
of jamming on instruments back in the White Eskimo
days were inspiring him to get involved with the new
songs on a musical as well as lyrical level. He could
hold his own in a songwriting session on guitar and
piano, and so the Jamaican studio sessions began to
become productive, with an album's worth of songs
slowly coming together.

In case you're wondering if the evenings after the
studio work were one long party, let it be known that
the band's downtime was largely devoted to watching
rom-coms on Netflix in the evening. Harry knew that
there was work to be done…

Harry accepts the ARIA award for Best International Act in
Australia, 2017.

Meeting the fans in
Australia: too much of this
would have anyone looking
like a rabbit in headlights.

Test your Harry knowledge!

CAN YOU HIT THE GOLDEN NOTE?

Q1: What is Harry's record label called?

Q2: Where did Harry go to unwind after 1D split?

Q3: When was Harry's first solo album released?

Grab a notepad and pen and see how well you know Harry.
Answers on p122

Harry Styles
The album

THE BOY BECOMES A MAN WITH HIS EXCELLENT, SADLY-NOT-PINK SOLO ALBUM

The worst thing Harry could have done when he was writing and recording his first solo album would have been to make it sound like One Direction. If the music had been less cool than 1D's, he would have been doomed; if it had been better, people would have said, "Not as good as the old days."

Fortunately, our man knew this perfectly well and unleashed an album that was part-rock, part-pop, part-old and part-new – and wholly unexpected, at least by the younger fans who had been following him since he first got famous in 2010. There were mature concepts running through the *Harry Styles* album – with its slightly boring title chosen by the record company over his first choice, Pink – that would have made even a far more experienced songwriter proud.

One of these was a song cycle about relationships, a subject that often reared its head in interviews: this was partly to do with the song 'Two Ghosts'. Harry had written this track with Julian Bunetta and John Ryan in

Looking pretty intense on *The X Factor* in Italy.

58

Harry Styles: the album

Guitar man: Harry performs at the We Can Survive show at the Hollywood Bowl in California.

" Harry unleashed an album that was part-rock, part-pop, part-old and part-new"

2013, but held onto it for later improvement, and its line 'same lips red, same eyes blue' seemed to be a clear reference to Harry's ex, Taylor Swift, who we'll be talking about later on. Radio 1's Nick Grimshaw pressed Harry about this on his show, to which the singer was audibly uncomfortable, asking his manager, Jeffrey Azoff, to help him out. "I think it's pretty self-explanatory," he mumbled, the situation not being helped by Swift's own song 'Style' on the *1989* album of 2014.

Musically, 'Two Ghosts' was a departure for Harry, with elements of soft and classic rock in its sound – almost as if his parents' interest in Seventies' bands such as Fleetwood Mac and Pink Floyd had been on his mind. Then there

Test your Harry knowledge!

CAN YOU HIT THE GOLDEN NOTE?

Q1: Which Radio 1 DJ quizzed Harry on air?

Q2: What was the album's first single called?

Q3: In which American city did Harry kick off his debut concert tour in 2017?

Grab a notepad and pen and see how well you know Harry.
Answers on p122

> ❝ **I wanted to write my stories, things that happened to me. I wanted to be honest**❞

was the first single, 'Sign Of The Times', with an intro that owed a lot to David Bowie's 'Space Oddity', and the Fleet Foxes-indebted 'Meet Me In The Hallway'. Guitar and piano artists such as The Rolling Stones, Elton John and Stealers Wheel arguably made their presence felt too, but in gentle homage rather than through being shamelessly ripped off.

As Harry told *Rolling Stone*, his first solo record was intended to showcase what he could do when he wasn't being ordered around as part of a band. "I didn't want to write 'stories'," he said. "I wanted to write my stories, things that happened to me. The number one thing was I wanted to be honest. I hadn't done that before… I wanted to step up. There were songs I wanted to write and record, and not just have it be 'Here's a demo I wrote'. Every decision I've made since I was 16 was made in a democracy. I felt like it was time to make a decision about the future – and maybe I shouldn't rely on others."

One thing was for sure: with *Harry Styles*, our hero had marked out his path – and it was not the one everybody expected. Respect is due to Harry for that.

Harry walks the runway at the 2017 Victoria's Secret Fashion Show in Shanghai.

With a few close friends at the Mercedes-Benz Arena in Shanghai, China.

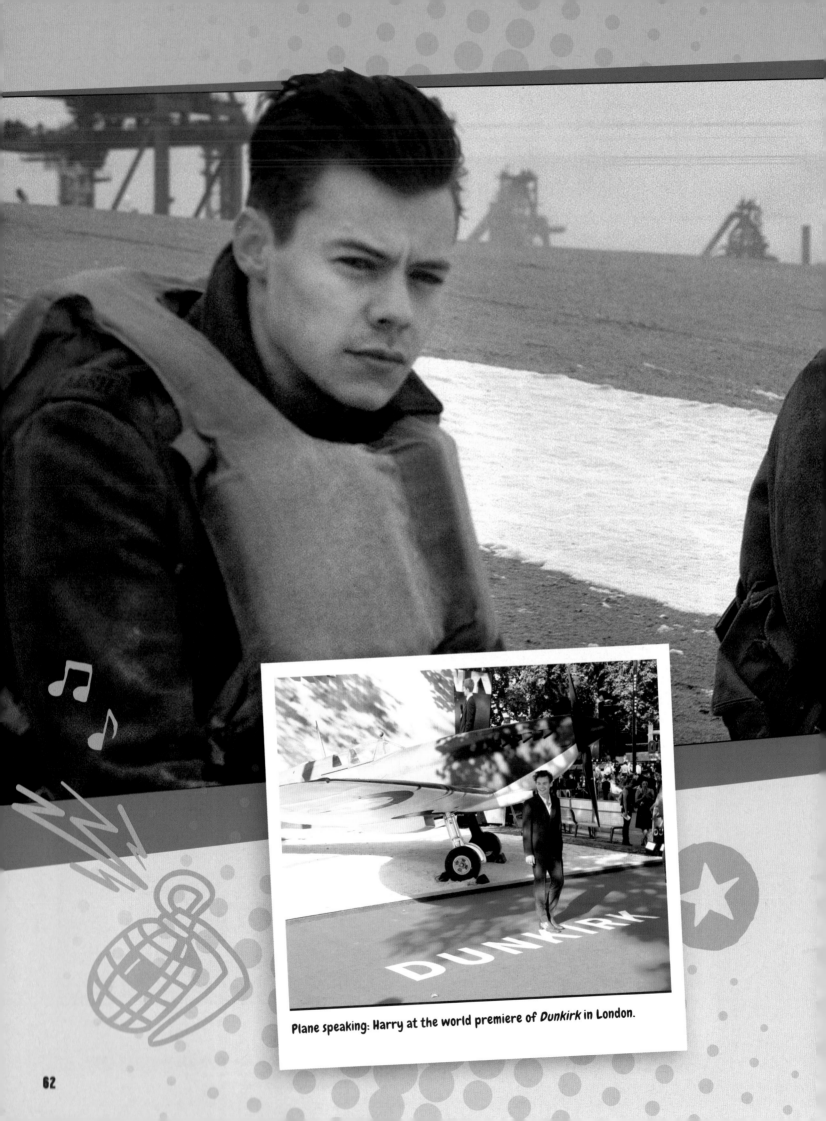

Plane speaking: Harry at the world premiere of *Dunkirk* in London.

Harry (left) on the beaches with *Dunkirk* co-stars Aneurin Barnard and Fionn Whitehead.

Dunkirk

ACTING UP: WHEN HARRY DEBUTED ON THE BIG SCREEN IN A TRUE WAR EPIC

f you have a year off between the split of your band and your debut album, how do you spend your time? Why, acting in a big-budget Hollywood movie, of course.

Harry pulled off the neat trick in 2016 of acting in a film that was a) really good, b) offered him a cool part that he didn't mess up, and c) got great reviews. Many a veteran movie actor would give a kidney to be guaranteed those three advantages, but Harry really lucked out with Christopher Nolan's World War II epic, *Dunkirk*. "The movie is so ambitious," he said. "Some of the stuff they're doing in this movie is insane. And it was hard, physically really tough, but I love acting. I love playing someone else. I'd sleep really well at night, then get up and continue drowning."

He was referring here to the ocean scenes in which his character, a soldier named Alex, found himself at various points in the film. Fortunately

Images: Alamy, Getty

63

Everybody shake - Harry at the film premiere in New York.

Test your Harry knowledge!

CAN YOU HIT THE GOLDEN NOTE?

🎵 **Q1:** What was the name of Harry's character?

🎵 **Q2:** How much did *Dunkirk* make at the box office?

🎵 **Q3:** How much did Harry earn for his role in *Dunkirk*?

Grab a notepad and pen and see how well you know Harry.
Answers on p122

Harry is a decent swimmer, and also he had chopped off his long hair for the role, meaning that he didn't have to walk around with sopping wet locks on set. Asked about his short back and sides haircut, he mused: "We had to make the chop. I felt very naked but it was good! It's very breezy."

Interestingly, Harry had to audition with every other aspiring actor who wanted the role. His talent representatives, Creative Artists Agency (CAA), sent a tape of Harry acting to Nolan's casting director and he was invited along to a workshop audition. Harry knew Nolan's previous films, *The Dark Knight Trilogy* and *Memento* in particular: of the latter, he said, "I always found his structure so interesting, in terms of the way he keeps stuff from the audience when the characters don't know about it – and it hits you so much harder."

Many of the other actors knew who Harry was, but Nolan himself didn't have a clue: as he later said, "My daughter had talked about him, but I wasn't really that aware of it. I cast Harry because he fit the part wonderfully and truly earned a seat at the table… He has the kind of face that makes you believe he could have been alive in that period."

The movie was shot in northern France between July and September 2016, where Harry had to swim in the sea wearing an overcoat and carrying a pack. At the end of his first day, Nolan turned to Harry and said, "Congrats on your first close-up." The praise was earned: Harry worked hard on his lines, which were mostly short sentences, including "For f***'s sake!" and "If he does, it's in an accent thicker than sauerkraut sauce."

Some of the shoot was genuinely hard work, as he later recalled, "There was a boat blowing up as you were swimming, there were bullet noises everywhere, there was fire, people screaming… There was a lot going on. There was a bit where you're like, are we filming? What just happened?" Of a long underwater scene, he explained, "While you're down there filming and acting out the scene, you're also thinking, 'I cannot breathe for much longer.'"

His efforts paid off, with *The Independent* writing, 'Styles is very competent and his performance does not stick out like a sore thumb as many feared'. *Rolling Stone* observed that he played a small role with 'subtle grace and zero pop star showboating'. As for the public reaction – they lined up to see *Dunkirk*, helping it to earn $522 million worldwide against a budget of $100 million. Not a bad way to make your debut in the movie industry, right?

The veteran actor Mark Rylance and Harry at the afterparty for the premiere in NYC.

See yourself here? Then you're a true Styles fan and one of a very cool gang!

Harry's fans

HARRY STYLES FANS ARE THE BEST IN THE WORLD – BUT THERE ARE A LOT OF US. HOW DOES HE HANDLE ALL THE ADORATION?

No one knows the boy-band phenomenon better than a former boy-band star, and so it was for Ronan Keating a few years back. The some-time Boyzone heart-throb for millions, whose music – like that of One Direction, if not quite as evolved – was inescapable through most of the Nineties, was arriving at Heathrow on a flight from Los Angeles. Observing hundreds of screaming fans, he chuckled in amusement: "Sadly not for me, ha ha! One Direction were on the flight… Those were the days!"

Make no mistake, Harry's fans can make a noise as loud or louder than any former tribe of pop-star followers, whether that's the legions who adored The Beatles in the Sixties, the Bay City Rollers in the Seventies, Duran Duran in the Eighties, or Take That in the Nineties. A writer, *Hollywood Life*'s Dory Larrabee-Zayas, wrote of these devotees, "I saw so many girls crying so hard, they looked like they were in pain, but they were tears of joy."

From the moment Harry appeared on *The X Factor* for the first time, his house in Holmes

Meeting the fans in Venice. If they get too close, they'll get poked by those collars.

Images: Getty Images

67

Chapel was besieged. Hundreds of young people gathered outside his family home in the town's London Road, calling his name. In later years, when Harry's mum Anne married Robin Twist, there was no choice but to create a full-on fake bus, with fake wedding guests on board, to drive off to Doncaster racecourse – a full 80 miles away from the real wedding venue – to give Harry's fans the slip.

But this doesn't mean that Harry has no time for his fans. The opposite is true: he admires them, and takes their views seriously. As he once explained, "Who's to say that young girls who like pop music – short for popular, right? – have worse musical taste than a 30-year-old hipster guy? That's not up to you to say. Music is something that's always changing. There's no goal posts. Young girls like The Beatles. You gonna tell me they're not serious? How can you say young girls don't get it? They're our future. Our future doctors, lawyers, mothers, presidents, they kind of keep the world going. Teenage-girl fans – they don't lie. If they like you, they're there. They don't act 'too cool'. They like you, and they tell you."

Nowadays, busloads of Harry fans regularly make the journey to Holmes Chapel, where there are a few absolute landmarks that they have to visit. The first of these is Harry's aforementioned house on the London Road. His family no longer live there, but it's still inhabited – the new owners must have been quite surprised by the attention paid to their modest dwelling when they moved in.

Then there's the Fortune City Chinese restaurant, just down the road: Harry has always mentioned it as his favourite dining spot when he was a kid. After that, fans like to take in the W. Mandeville bakery, where Harry used to work and which sports a life-sized placard of him, holding a loaf of bread and laughing. Finally, Harry's followers like to walk 20 minutes along Macclesfield Road to the Twemlow railway viaduct where Harry famously wrote his name in the *This Is Us* film. See you there!

A spot of rain doesn't deter the most loyal fans on Planet Pop.

Test your Harry knowledge!

CAN YOU HIT THE GOLDEN NOTE?

Q1: What road is Harry's old family home on?

Q2: Where did Harry famously write his name?

Q3: What are Harry's fans often called?

Grab a notepad and pen and see how well you know Harry.
Answers on p122

The famous Twemlow Viaduct where Harry wrote his name. Have you written yours there?

" Busloads of Harry fans regularly make the journey to Holmes Chapel, where there are landmarks that they have to visit"

Fashion

HOW THE KID FROM HOLMES CHAPEL BECAME THE FACE OF MEN'S FASHION

We tend to think of our pop stars as pretty open-minded when it comes to what they wear, don't we? But take a closer look at the average boy band and consider what they're wearing. Since the dawn of time (around 1988), all boy bands have worn a) sports footwear, b) a T-shirt, sometimes with a logo, c) jeans, baggy or skinny, and d) an accessory such as a bandana or oversized jewellery. The uniform hasn't actually changed that much over the decades.

Harry Styles has done more than most of his colleagues in boy-band world to push that envelope out and generate a look of his own. As a teenager, he loved the obvious Ray-Bans, Adidas and Nike trainers, and Ralph Lauren polo shirts, but that soon changed. In the One Direction days, he was often seen stepping out in a skin-tight black outfit when the other four were sporting the usual leisurewear. Of course, that is about as far as he could go when he was a member of the band: you need to show unity with your bandmates for marketing reasons – but once he was out on his own, he was free to wear whatever he wanted.

And didn't he just… notable outfits that we've seen outside the Styles physique have featured long-collar blouses and bows, trousers both skin-tight and generously bell-bottomed, jackets and suits of all shades of the rainbow – and more. He's an exhibitionist at heart, as we discovered when he paraded

Sometimes it's all about being casual: Harry leaving BBC Radio 2 in February 2020.

The style of Styles: Harry and the designer Alessandro Michele at the Metropolitan Museum of Art in New York in 2019.

Images: Getty Images

around *The X Factor* house in only a gold leopard-print thong, and if there's a fashion show on any given night and he's in the area, he'll be there.

Notable catwalk sightings have seen Harry alongside James Corden at the 2012 London Fashion Week at the Savoy Hotel, where he wore a beige Aquascutum trenchcoat supplied by the evening's main brand, as well as the following year's event. On that occasion, he sat with Nick Grimshaw, Kelly Osbourne and Nicola Roberts at Henry Holland's runway show at Somerset House – and this time he wore a plain, white T-shirt to convey his neutrality.

On the same evening, he sat with supermodels Suki Waterhouse and Sienna Miller, and was quizzed by the media about his supposed relationship with another model, Cara Delevingne, to which he snapped, "She's not my girl. I know what you're doing." In protest, he donned a black balaclava with the letters BS written in white across the top, to make his feelings clear.

Harry occasionally makes his own fashion designs – such as the hoodie he designed with three pictures of Alain de Botton across the front – and has been given many awards for his style, no pun intended. He was the first man to win the British Style Award at the British Fashion Awards, described as, 'embodying the spirit of London' and as 'an international ambassador for London as a leading creative fashion capital'. Over the years he's worn suits from Yves Saint Laurent and Gucci, and even employs his own stylist, Harry Lambert, who produced the floral suit he wore to the 2015 American Music Awards.

It's all a long way from the hightops and baggy jeans Harry wore in the Holmes Chapel days, isn't it? Long may his trip down the fashion runway continue, we say.

Mellow yellow: Harry ensuring visibility at the Brit Awards in 2020.

> " Harry occasionally makes his own fashion designs, and has been given many awards for his style, no pun intended"

Test your Harry knowledge!

CAN YOU HIT THE GOLDEN NOTE?

♪ **Q1:** What did Harry write on his balaclava?

♪ **Q2:** What's Harry's stylist called?

♪ **Q3:** True or false: he was the first man to appear solo on the cover of *Vogue*?

Grab a notepad and pen and see how well you know Harry.
Answers on p122

Checking out: Harry in a suit that owes its design to many popular tea-towels.

Mercedes-B

Fine Line

ALBUM TWO FOR THE SOLO STYLES STEPPED ACROSS A FEW LINES, FINE AND OTHERWISE

There is heartbreak and humour aplenty on *Fine Line*, which was released on 13 December 2019. For a dose of the former, check 'Falling', which is almost certainly about Harry's painful break up with Camille Rowe: the lyrics mention a coffee at the Beachwood Cafe in the Hollywood Hills, where Camille frequently visited. Then there's 'Cherry', on which Camille actually speaks via a message on Harry's voicemail, and which has the line, 'Does he take you walking round his parents' gallery?', presumably a reference to Camille's new boyfriend Theo Niarchos, a member of the Los Angeles art community. Finally, there's 'To Be So Lonely', a mournful tune in which Harry berates himself for being arrogant and unable to apologise. This is sad stuff by anyone's standards.

Harry's ex, Camille Rowe, an inspiration for three *Fine Line* songs, at the Paris Fashion Week in 2018.

Fortunately, Harry knows better than to wallow in misery, and there's plenty of upbeat material to enjoy on *Fine Line*. The title track came out of a simple guitar-strumming session between him and his fellow songwriter, Tom Hull, and he described it as, "one of those songs that I've always wanted to make." Then there's 'Golden', a soft-rock song that he described as "feeling so Malibu," referring to the California beach rather than the popular coconut drink. Songs such as these reveal Harry's keen interest in classic folk-rock albums, such as 1968's *Astral Weeks* by Van Morrison and Joni Mitchell's *Blue* LP of 1971.

The song 'Canyon Moon' takes Harry's Joni obsession to its logical limit, as he decided to use a dulcimer – a stringed folk instrument – like the one she played on *Blue*. He tracked down the maker of the original instrument, Joellen Lapidus, in Culver City, California, and purchased one identical to the dulcimer that Lapidus had sold to Joni at the Big Sur Folk Festival in 1969. It's a beautiful-sounding instrument, and about as far from One Direction as you can get, incidentally.

Another highlight of *Fine Line* is 'Treat People With Kindness', which Harry had apparently been reluctant to write in case it came across as cynically cashing in on a slogan. In fact 'TPWK' is an uplifting track with choral elements that has

Fresh fruit for everyone: Harry in November 2019 in Los Angeles.

> **It's a beautiful-sounding instrument, and about as far from One Direction as you can get**

Test your Harry knowledge!

CAN YOU HIT THE GOLDEN NOTE?

Q1: Which ex inspired three songs on *Fine Line*?

Q2: What does TPWK stand for?

Q3: Who co-starred in the video for Harry's 'Treat People With Kindness' single?

Grab a notepad and pen and see how well you know Harry.
Answers on p122

a simple, important message. As he explained, "It's about being a lot nicer to each other than, 'Don't do this, or don't do that...' it's just saying 'Treat people with kindness.'"

No fewer than seven singles came from *Fine Line*, such was the appetite among Styles fans for new material. These were 'Lights Up', 'Adore You', 'Falling', 'Watermelon Sugar', 'Golden', 'Treat People With Kindness', and the title track itself, and it was no surprise when the album entered the UK Albums Chart at Number 3. In the USA, it went straight in at Number 1, becoming Harry's second album in a row to do so – it even seemed at that point that he might defeat One Direction's record in that regard. Since then, *Fine Line* has gone triple platinum in the USA, taking physical sales and album-equivalent units into account.

If there was any doubt that Harry could pull off a career as a solo artist, it was dispelled by now. What lay ahead?

Jamming with the great Stevie Nicks at the 2019 Rock & Roll Hall Of Fame Induction Ceremony in New York.

A moment in time: John Sebastian, Graham Nash, Harry's idol Joni Mitchell, David Crosby and Stephen Stills on stage at the 1969 Big Sur Folk Festival.

On tour

"Although Harry doesn't have an entourage, he seeks out interesting people to hang out with when he's on the road"

ON THE ROAD, ON THE STAGE AND ON THE PLANE: WHAT'S IT LIKE TO TOUR THE WORLD WHEN YOU'RE HARRY STYLES?

Times have changed for pop stars on tour: today's backstage world is less about sex, drugs and rock'n'roll and more about accountants' meetings, green tea and working out. It has to be this way: unlike the bad old days of the Seventies to the Nineties, everything a celeb does now is on camera and on social media; legal agreements keep mouths closed and lawyers rich; and there's so much money flowing that any element of legal or physical risk is removed from the situation.

This is not necessarily a bad thing, because the average dressing-room is a healthier place to be than it was 40 years ago – but at the same time, you have to ask yourself if today's pop star actually has any fun on tour.

In the case of Harry Styles, the answer is definitely yes. Although he doesn't have an entourage, he seeks out interesting people to hang out with when he's on the road. Remember the time he had a night of drinking with Ed Sheeran, and the two guys decided to go and get a tattoo together? Or the time when One Direction all went to a casino in Perth, Western Australia, during the *Up All Night* tour. All five played several hours of roulette, except Niall, who won £100 and quit, watching the others lose their money. "Let's just say a lot of money was lost. A lot!" he chuckled. "When

A host of tour buses are needed to get bands from one show to the next. Which one would you choose?

Tripping the light fantastic:
Harry performs at Radio City
Music Hall in 2017 in New York.

Images: Getty Images

Ringing in the chords on stage: Harry smiles for his fans.

management found out, we got a serious dressing down."

Of course, you can't do this every night, not when a huge tour looms ahead of you. Look at the sheer numbers of the Take Me Home tour, which included 123 shows across the globe, with concerts in the US, Japan and Australia, and six nights at the London O2 Arena. More than 300,000 tickets were sold for the UK and Ireland shows in one day, while no fewer than 108,000 fans went to see 1D play at the Foro Sol stadium in Mexico City. The tour brought in well over $100 million, leading Andy Greene, an associate editor with *Rolling Stone* magazine, to comment: "It's insane; they're working them like dogs and printing money right now."

The key point in Greene's comment was about money. When this much cash is coming in, no band can be drunk or high all the time, or at all, really: too much is riding on their performances. People need a break, though, and Simon Cowell understood that 1D needed to party sometimes or the band would suffer. He once said, "They're good-looking guys and they all like girls," although that didn't permit liaisons with the 1D staff. As Lou Teasdale, who looked after make-up and style on One Direction's tours, explained: "You can't sleep with them. It's kind of important if you want to keep your job."

Where does Harry fit into all this? Well, he's a friendly guy and will always stop to talk to fans, but for a few years now he's been focusing on his health while on tour. He once went on a juice cleanse in LA, admitting that he had been feeling 'gross' after flying so much on tour, and he also took up yoga and Pilates to help with a bad back, exacerbated by dancing around a stage every night for months on end.

Good for him. With healthy priorities like that, he'll be around to entertain us for many years to come.

Images: Getty Images

Test your Harry knowledge!

CAN YOU HIT THE GOLDEN NOTE?

Q1: Which 1D member won £100 at roulette?

Q2: How much money did the Take Me Home tour generate?

Q3: How many shows were in the Live on Tour schedule?

Grab a notepad and pen and see how well you know Harry.
Answers on p122

Viva Las Vegas: Harry's Love On Tour concert at MGM Grand Garden Arena in Nevada, 2021.

Small screen

YOU DON'T NEED TO GO TO THE CINEMA TO SEE HARRY. HE'S RIGHT THERE ON YOUR TV!

f you search YouTube for Harry Styles, you get more than 30 million results, which – assuming each one lasts a couple of minutes – would take you 100 years to watch, so any article examining Harry's presence on your phone or computer screen is doomed to fail. Ask us about Harry on TV, though, and we can cover a lot of ground quite quickly, although you'll have to exclude music awards shows that have been broadcast on telly or we'll be here all day.

The X Factor 2010 was obviously the first time that any of us saw Harry's smiling face on TV, and when One Direction became stratospherically famous, they were all over every British talk show you want to mention. Streaming video wasn't really a thing back then, and YouTube was far less powerful than it is now, so people still tuned in en masse to see broadcast programmes at allotted times. How quaint!

An early TV highlight was Alan Carr's show *Chatty Man*, on which the host asked Harry about his rumoured relationship with model Madison McMillin. "Did you take a trip down Madison Avenue?" quipped Carr. Later TV appearances with Piers Morgan and then on *The Alan Titchmarsh Show* followed a similar line of questioning, to Harry's embarrassment.

American TV has generally been more supportive. In 2012, One Direction made a cameo appearance in the teen drama *iCarly*, before delivering the first of three appearances on the veteran comedy show *Saturday Night Live* (*SNL*). Harry also appeared on *SNL* as a solo artist, notably in 2017, in a role that required serious comedy skills alongside the host Jimmy Fallon.

Smile, you're on camera: Harry at the Venice International Film Festival in Italy.

Harry with *The Late Late Show* host James Corden, a fellow British expat.

First, he was required to sing 'Let's Dance' by David Bowie during Fallon's opening monologue, before doing an impression of the Rolling Stones' singer Mick Jagger in a skit called Celebrity Family Feud. Expertly mocking himself, he said in a perfect Jagger accent: "Why would anyone in a successful band go solo? That is insane!" He finished the show by donning a fake beard and acting a Confederate soldier's role in a Civil War sketch, in which an old folk song turns into a boy-band performance. His stick-on beard falling off was an unexpected bonus.

Harry also fielded a slight dig on Ellen DeGeneres' self-titled talk show when, in a segment called Never Have I Ever, he was presented with, "Never have I ever made out with someone double my age." Quipping, "What is this game?" in good humour, he avoided the subject – of Caroline Flack, presumably – very neatly.

Harry has also enjoyed a long on- and off-screen friendship and collaboration with the British TV host James Corden, on whose *Late Late Show* he has memorably appeared. On one Corden skit, Tattoo Roulette, Harry and Niall competed, with the loser promising to have 'Late Late' tattooed on him: Harry lost. On Corden's famous Carpool Karaoke, Harry, Liam, Louis and the host himself sang 'What Makes You Beautiful', 'Story Of My Life', 'No Control', 'Perfect' and 'Drag Me Down'.

The cast of *iCarly* at Nickelodeon Studios in Burbank, California. One Direction made an appearance on the show early in their career.

On *The Tonight Show Starring Jimmy Fallon* at Rockefeller Center on 19 July 2017 in New York.

Test your Harry knowledge!

CAN YOU HIT THE GOLDEN NOTE?

Q1: Which model did Alan Carr ask Harry about?

Q2: Which famous rocker did Harry impersonate?

Q3: Which US sketch comedy show has Harry featured on as both a guest and a host?

Grab a notepad and pen and see how well you know Harry.

Answers on p122

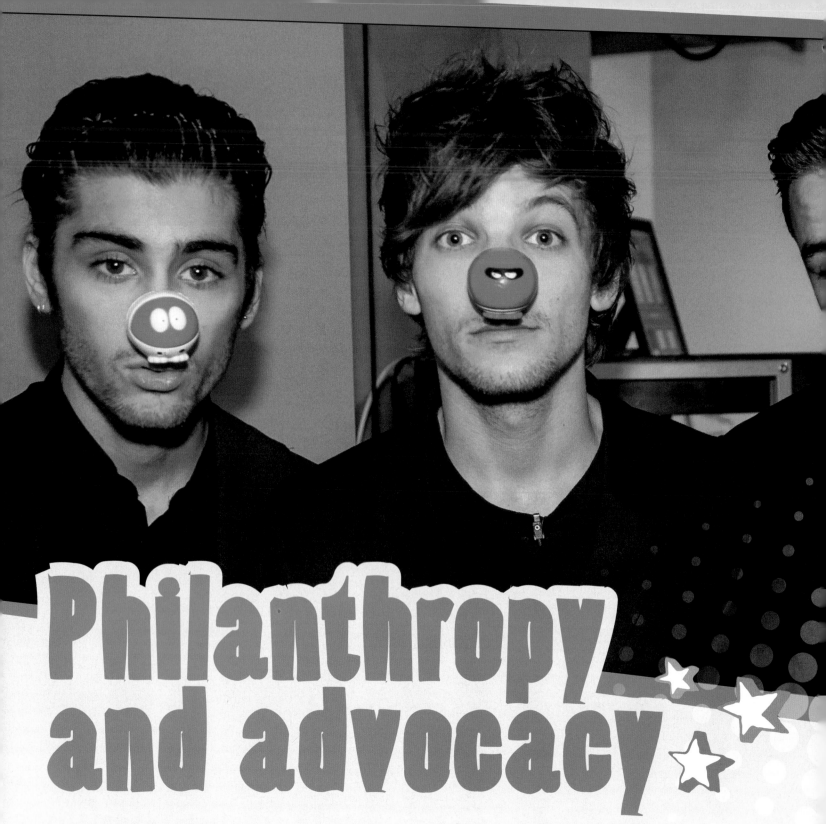

Philanthropy and advocacy

HOW HARRY HAS HELPED AND PROMOTED A RANGE OF SOCIALLY BENEFICIAL CAUSES

Charitable causes have always been part and parcel of Harry's creative endeavours, whether as a solo artist, with One Direction, or as part of a larger collective of musicians. The first of these came as early as 2010, when he and 1D collaborated on an *X Factor* charity single that raised money for the armed forces charity Help For Heroes. Their song was a version of David Bowie's anthemic 'Heroes'.

In 2013, One Direction were involved in that year's Comic Relief campaign, which ultimately raised more than £100 million for various causes. Rather than simply donating money, 1D flew to Accra, the capital of the African country of Ghana, where they filmed a series of video diaries. These clips, revealing the inadequacy of the city's medical facilities, are hard to watch: at one point Harry is seen in tears, witnessing the sight of a baby suffering from malaria.

"If you get involved in it and you don't cry, then you're superhuman," he said, accurately. "We thought we knew what it's like, but when you're there and you get the smells, your eyes hurt from the smoke, you cough, you're feeling it all."

As the years passed, Directioners got on board with these causes. On Harry's birthday, they

Zayn, Louis, Liam, Harry and Niall on Red Nose Day at the London Palladium in 2015.

will often make a donation in his name, on one occasion giving more than £5,000 to the Believe In Magic charity, simply to celebrate another trip around the sun for their hero. He ramped up his own activities in this area, being well able to afford to do so but also motivated by the sights he'd seen as he travelled the world: a given Harry tour always donates to charities at tour stops along the way. These have included Safe Place For Youth in California; children's cancer research in Switzerland, Denmark and Norway; refugee support in Germany; and food banks in Holland, Spain and Italy.

Real progress can only be made in the charitable sector if the causes of society's ills are addressed at their root, and Harry recognised

On stage during the fifth annual 'We Can Survive' benefit concert in 2017 in Hollywood.

Images: Getty Images

Return of the Mac: Lindsey Buckingham of Fleetwood Mac and Harry at MusiCares Person of the Year ceremony in 2018 in New York.

this early on, stating that he wanted to support what he called the 'fundamentals' of good human behaviour. In 2018, for instance, he signed a petition in support of March for Our Lives, the Washington, DC protest that demanded stricter gun control after the mass shooting at Marjory Stoneman Douglas High School in Florida that year. He also made two flags part of his stage show, the first bearing the Black Lives Matter symbol and the other a rainbow for the Pride movement. Meanwhile, his 'Treat People With Kindness' T-shirts raised funds for the educational charity GLSEN, or Gay, Lesbian and Straight Education Network.

Even just by appearing at charitable events – such as the annual pre-Grammys MusiCares Person of the Year night, as he did in 2018 – Harry is helping to raise awareness that work needs to be done to improve life in all sectors of our society. You can do your bit, too. Keep an eye out for Harry's charitable efforts, and do what you can to help him.

Test your Harry knowledge!

CAN YOU HIT THE GOLDEN NOTE?

Q1: How much did 1D help raise for Comic Relief in 2013?

Q2: Which African country did Harry visit?

Q3: Harry's first tour raised $1.2m for charity – True or False?

Grab a notepad and pen and see how well you know Harry.
Answers on p122

Signed guitars from Machine Gun Kelly and Harry on display at Julien's Auctions in Beverly Hills, California, in 2021.

'End Gun Violence' was the message on Harry's guitar at New York's Madison Square Garden in 2018 – and why not? It's perfectly possible.

Treat People With Kindness

BEHIND THE TPWK SLOGAN – AND WHY IT'S MORE IMPORTANT THAN YOU THINK

In the last decade, the issues of gender politics and mental health, and how those two subjects intersect at a place of tolerance and acceptance, have been at the forefront of young people's conversations – and not a moment too soon. Progression in those areas has been highlighted and assisted by the efforts of high-profile stars such as Harry Styles, making those issues more visible

and – we hope, at least – making life easier for anyone struggling for clarity and identity. This is why his slogan 'Treat People With Kindness' has been so important.

The four-word phrase began life as a song on 2019's *Fine Line* album, of course, and generally abbreviated to 'TPWK' afterwards. A glorious few minutes of musical drama, the song distilled the idea that being supportive of other people is generally a sensible

Fans showing their appreciation of Harry and his messaging at Rockefeller Plaza in New York in 2020.

Images: Getty Images

91

thing to do if we all want to make a better world for ourselves, and the title soon took on a higher meaning. From 2019 on, we could see those four letters on a badge on Harry's guitar straps, and he soon commissioned a range of T-shirts bearing the slogan for sale at his shows. They eventually formed part of a charitable fundraising drive that raised millions of pounds.

Harry could have stopped there, having made his point, but he took the idea much further. He founded a website for World Mental Health Day called 'Do You Know Who You Are', where visitors could enter their name and receive a personal compliment from Harry to get their day off to a good start. He also responded personally to an online post from a fan who planned to skip therapy to come to his next tour. He told her: "Go to therapy, it's important. I'll wait for you."

During a concert at the Ericsson Globe in Stockholm, Harry told the crowd: "I love every single one of you: if you are black, if you are white, if you are gay, if you are straight, if you are transgender – whoever you are, whoever you want to be – I support you. I love every single one of you."

At another show, this time at the SAP Center in San Jose, California, Harry put the concert on hold for a moment when he spotted one of the audience holding up a sign that read, "I'm gonna come out to my parents because of you." He asked the young woman, who was called Grace, if he could read it out to the crowd, and then asked her the name of her mother. Hearing that Grace's mother was named Tina, he asked the entire crowd to shout, "Tina, she's gay!"

Grace later stated: "Harry is a proud supporter of the LGBTQ+ community and he's made a lot of fans feel comfortable and proud to be who they are, and I'm just one example of that." If only more acts of his stature performed the same service for their fans, the world might be a better – and safer – place.

The bond between Harry and his fans is real, as is the surprise on the blue-shirted guy's face.

Attendees at a Pride parade, demonstrating that Harry's message resonated with them.

Test your Harry knowledge!

CAN YOU HIT THE GOLDEN NOTE?

Q1: What was the name of Harry's pro-mental heath website?

Q2: What was the fan in San Jose called?

Q3: On what album did TPWK make its debut?

Grab a notepad and pen and see how well you know Harry.
Answers on p122

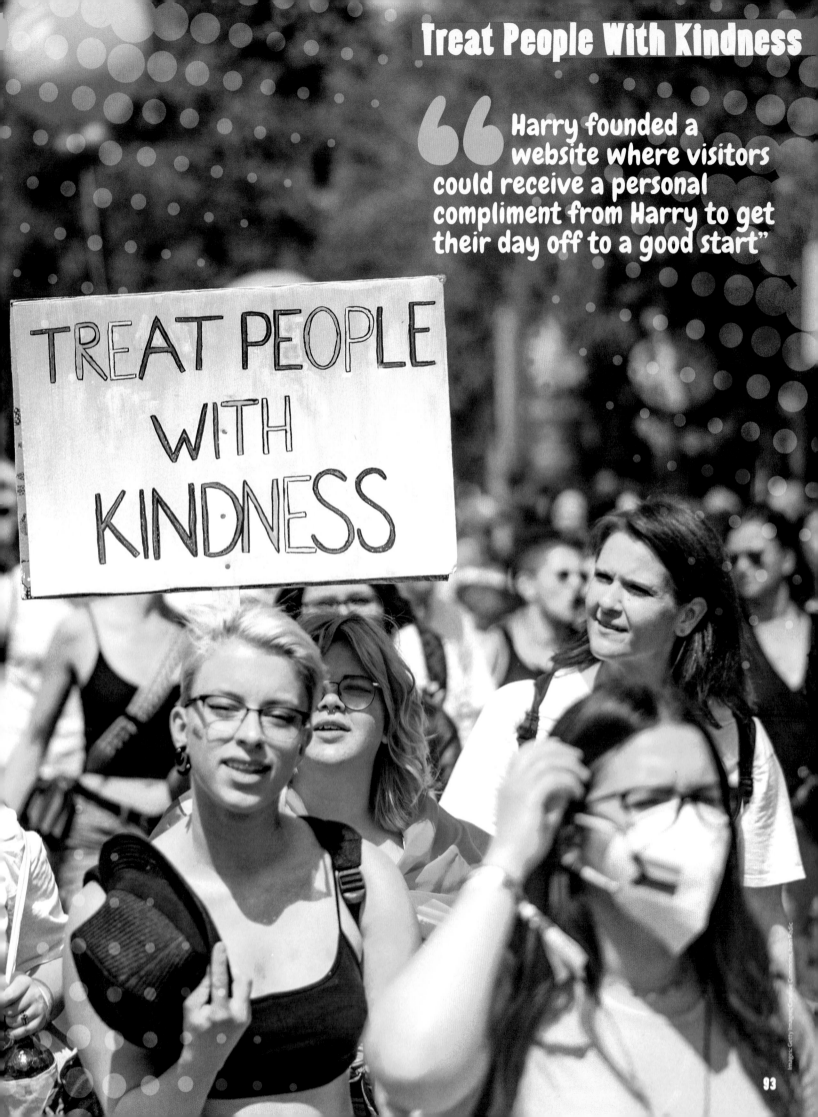

" Harry founded a website where visitors could receive a personal compliment from Harry to get their day off to a good start"

TREAT PEOPLE WITH KINDNESS

Personal life

WE KNOW THE MUSICIAN. WE KNOW THE PERFORMER. WE KNOW THE SONGWRITER – BUT DO WE REALLY KNOW THE MAN?

So, what do we know about the life of Harry Styles when he's out of the public eye?

At the time of writing in late 2022, he splits his time between two homes, both in North London. He also has an apartment in Manhattan, but got rid of his Los Angeles home a while back. A quick visit to Companies House reveals that Harry has four active company directorships: just one of these, Erskine Records, revealed assets of around £30 million in each of the last two tax years, from which we can reasonably infer that he spends a fair bit of time dealing with accountants, investment managers and so on. His private life isn't all about sipping cocktails by the pool.

Still, given his personal fortune in 2022 of around £100 million, Harry is able to enjoy himself, and so he does, having built fine art and fashion collections. He was declared Britain's wealthiest musician under 30 this year – and on that note, with the big 3-0 approaching in 2024, Harry spends a lot of time on his mental and physical health, making sure with the

Taylor Swift and Harry walking in Central Park in 2012 – but did he share his sweets with her?

The late Caroline Flack, pictured here in 2011: Harry had a brief relationship with the *X Factor* presenter.

help of yoga, Pilates, therapy, meditation and a pescatarian diet that he avoids the dreaded middle-age spread that has curtailed many a slim young star's career.

Harry isn't a religious man as such, but he told one interviewer that he is "more spiritual than religious," and that it is "naïve to say nothing exists and there's nothing above us or more powerful than us." Does he have any bad habits at all? It seems not, the occasional shot of tequila or glass of wine aside.

With all that said, Harry's love life could take up this entire publication, so let's sum up by saying

Harry is able to enjoy himself, and so he does, having built fine art and fashion collections"

Images: Getty Images

95

"Fancy meeting you here!"
Harry and Kendall Jenner at
the Metropolitan Museum of
Art in 2019.

> **Harry had girlfriends at school, and has since been connected with many well-known women"**

Harry and his current partner, Olivia Wilde, doing a spot of shopping in London.

that he won't categorise his sexual orientation ("it's about not having to label everything, not having to clarify what boxes you're checking."). He has referred to having had girlfriends at school, and since fame came calling he has been connected with many well-known women. The first of these was a brief fling with *The X Factor* host Caroline Flack, which raised a few eyebrows as she was 31 at the time, while he was only 17. Sadly, Caroline took her own life in 2020. He then enjoyed an even briefer liaison with Taylor Swift, which generated several gazillion headlines and is thought to have inspired later songwriting by both stars.

A year-long relationship with French-American model Camille Rowe followed in 2017, and a dalliance with Kim Kardashian's supermodel half-sister, Kendall Jenner, was next, although that didn't last long. "Relationships are hard, at any age," he mused in *Rolling Stone*. "In writing songs about stuff like that, I like tipping a hat to the time together. You're celebrating the fact it was powerful and made you feel something, rather than 'This didn't work out, and that's bad'. And if you run into that person, maybe it's awkward, maybe you have to get drunk… but you shared something."

For the last two years, Harry has been in what appears to be a solid relationship with film director Olivia Wilde. Watch this space, but as he's now of dadhood age, wouldn't it be great if they had kids with the rock-star surname Wilde-Styles?

Test your Harry knowledge!

CAN YOU HIT THE GOLDEN NOTE?

Q1: How much is Harry's personal fortune in 2022?

Q2: Name his two preferred drinks.

Q3: What job does Olivia Wilde do?

Grab a notepad and pen and see how well you know Harry.
Answers on p122

> **Acclaimed as a musician, beloved as a performer, and praised for his songwriting, Harry pulled it all together for his third record"**

Harry's House

WITH HIS THIRD ALBUM, HARRY HAS COME INTO HIS OWN AS THE KEY PERFORMER OF HIS GENERATION. STEP INTO THE HOUSE!

Harry at the *My Policeman* première during the 2022 Toronto International Film Festival.

Haruomi Hosono, who inspired *Harry's House*, with the Best Original Music Award at the 13th Asian Film Awards in Hong Kong in 2019.

Harry's House, released on 20 May 2022, marks the point in Harry's career where everything converged in his favour. Acclaimed as a musician, beloved as a performer, and praised for his songwriting and activism, Harry pulled it all together for his third record, which enjoyed the best first-week sales of his career. It debuted at the top of the charts in the UK, the USA, Australia, Belgium, Canada, France, Germany, Ireland, Italy, the Netherlands, New Zealand, Spain, Sweden and Switzerland; sold more than half a million units in North America; and broke a record with four singles in the US Top 10 in the same week. Critics loved it, too. *Harry's House* was a success.

The album concept is appealing, which helped. As Harry explained to Apple Music, "The album is named after [the Japanese musician] Haruomi Hosono, he had an album in the Seventies called *Hosono House*… I heard that record and I was like, 'I love that. It'd be really fun to make a record called *Harry's House*.'"

The original idea, he added, was literally to record the music in his own home as per the title, but in the end the 'house' idea was more metaphorical than actual. "It was much more of an internal thing," he said. "It felt like it took on this whole new meaning and it was about, like: imagine, it's a day in my house, what do I go through?… In my house I'm playing fun music, sad music, I'm playing this, I'm playing that. It's a day in the life."

High points are many. The basic sound – a Japanese genre called 'city pop' – is upbeat, R&B-influenced and danceable, with inspiration taken from many sources. 'Matilda' is named after the Roald Dahl book of the same name, and is about a relationship Harry had with a troubled, unidentified person. "Sometimes it's just about listening. I hope that's what I did here," he told the radio DJ Zane Lowe. "If nothing else, it just says, 'I was listening to you'." Then there's 'Boyfriends', a dig into unsuccessful romantic alliances, and two songs that feature the American guitarist John Mayer, 'Cinema' and 'Daydreaming'.

The album was leaked a month before release, leading Sony Records to issue an angry tweet, but this seems not to have damaged its commercial performance. The single 'As It Was' appeared on 1 April, followed by 'Late Night Talking' on 21 June, and then 'Music For A Sushi Restaurant' on 3 October. All three singles performed phenomenally well, making 2022 The Year Of Harry Styles, in pop terms.

Musically, our man is unbeatable. This album marks the high point of Harry's career to date. While there is undoubtedly much excellent music left in him, the question is how long he can keep his music sharp, edgy and ahead of the curve, just as it is right now. Still, whatever happens next, we'll be with him all the way. This show isn't over yet.

"Gimme that notepad!" Some pop stars resent having to sign autographs. Not this one...

Harry accepts the Album of the Year award for *Harry's House* at the 2022 MTV Video Music Awards in New Jersey.

Test your Harry knowledge!

CAN YOU HIT THE GOLDEN NOTE?

Q1: Which Japanese songwriter inspired *Harry's House*?

Q2: Name the three singles from the album.

Q3: How long did 'As It Was' spend at Number 1 in the US?

Grab a notepad and pen and see how well you know Harry.
Answers on p122

Images: Getty Images

Harry starred alongside Florence Pugh and was directed by his partner Olivia Wilde in *Don't Worry Darling*.

Harry and *My Policeman* co-star Emma Corrin accept the TIFF Tribute Award for Performance at the TIFF Tribute Awards Gala.

Silver screen

HARRY HAS ALREADY APPEARED IN THREE FILM PRODUCTIONS. FANS LOVE HIS ACTING, BUT THE CRITICS AREN'T SURE. WHAT'S THE TRUTH?

Harry's fans gasped in amazement at the end of the 2021 movie *Eternals* when, in a mid-credits scene, their hero walked out of a tunnel dressed in a Marvel superhero costume and announced himself as Eros, brother of supervillain Thanos. He looked great, and hit his marks as instructed – but his accent, supposedly American but weaving back and forth to English and everywhere in between, was a bit of a mess. Still, that can be fixed…

The following year, Harry was back in cinemas in not one but two movies. The first, *Don't Worry Darling*, sees him alongside his real-life partner Olivia Wilde – who was also the director – plus Florence Pugh, Chris Pine and other known cinema names. The film's production was troubled, with actor Shia LaBeouf booted out by Wilde, and Harry taking his place, but once the furore died down, we could focus on our chap's performance. Warning: spoilers follow!

Test your Harry knowledge!

CAN YOU HIT THE GOLDEN NOTE?

♪ **Q1:** Who does Harry play in *Eternals*?

♪ **Q2:** Which English seaside resort is *My Policeman* set in?

♪ **Q3:** Which musical biopic did Harry audition for but not get cast?

Grab a notepad and pen and see how well you know Harry.
Answers on p122

Harry played the part of Jack Chambers, who lives with his wife, Alice (Pugh), in California. The couple are spied upon by Jack's boss, Frank (Pine), and a friend dies, leading the couple's relationship into turmoil: Alice eventually realises that they are living in a computer simulation. They fight, and she kills him before awakening in the real world. Sure, you might have seen some of this before in dozens of *Matrix*-indebted films, but what the heck, it's fun.

Reviews of Harry's acting were lukewarm: as Rotten Tomatoes put it, he gave 'a debatably entertaining turn', while Vulture.com said that he was 'not without talent but fails to give Jack the dimensionality or inner conflict the character clearly needs'. *The New Yorker* went too far when it said that Harry was 'utterly and helplessly adrift', though. The truth is that he did an acceptable job for a relatively inexperienced actor.

The second movie, *My Policeman*, was a smaller production but offered a better role for Harry. He plays a gay policeman,

Tom Burgess, who gets married in 1950s' Brighton to hide his sexuality. *The Hollywood Reporter* snootily said, 'He's not terrible, but he leaves a hole in the movie where a more multidimensional character with an inner life is needed most'. Indiewire said that the role 'requires levels of complexity and conveying inner turmoil that Styles can't provide'. And *Vanity Fair* wrote that, 'Styles's thoughtful, shaggy-sweet quality works well… but when he has to hold a scene's emotional tenor for longer than a line reading, he's flat'.

These were all reasonable conclusions, although the critics could have been a bit nicer about it. Harry is not without talent as an actor: he just needs time to mature into the craft, and some training wouldn't go amiss either. With perhaps a year spent at acting college, and some subtle, thoughtful roles to inhabit, he'll do just fine.

The bigger question is really whether any musician can transition to acting and still be taken seriously. Elvis Presley and Jon Bon Jovi couldn't do it. Frank Sinatra and Tom Waits absolutely could. Whose path will Harry follow?

Harry at the 79th Venice International Film Festival on the *Don't Worry Darling* red carpet.

In *My Policeman*, Harry starred alongside Emma Corrin as a gay policeman forced to marry to hide his sexuality in 1950s' Britain.

Role model

WHAT CAN WE LEARN FROM HARRY'S EXAMPLE? MORE THAN YOU MIGHT THINK...

What is a role model? It's someone who shows us what to do, how to behave and how to deal with life's challenges when they inevitably present themselves – to identify our 'role', and to show us how to fulfil it.

Such a person has to have conquered a certain number of obstacles and hindrances for us to take them seriously as a role model. We wouldn't trust the example of anyone who hadn't fought a few battles, would we? And as much as you might think, 'It's easy for Harry Styles – he's got £100 million, a pretty face and a fine art collection', that would indicate a failure to understand what it took him to get to that position.

First of all, understand that Harry didn't come from wealth, although he did possess assets of different kinds: a loving family, a decent education, and an upbringing that was relatively free of trauma, the early divorce of his parents Anne and Des aside. These gave him the confidence and the strength to try to enter the world of showbiz: to dare to fail, as the saying goes, because he had a support network to cushion him if – like a majority of all applicants – he failed to get through *The X Factor* auditions.

Beyond that support, though, Harry was on his own. He didn't have friends in the media who could give him a helping hand up. He didn't have a relative in the music industry who could give him a job, as Simon Cowell

The young Harry had the advantage of a loving family who would back him up in hard times.

You know what it's like when you land at an airport – you just want to get home. Now imagine being besieged by paparazzi in arrivals...

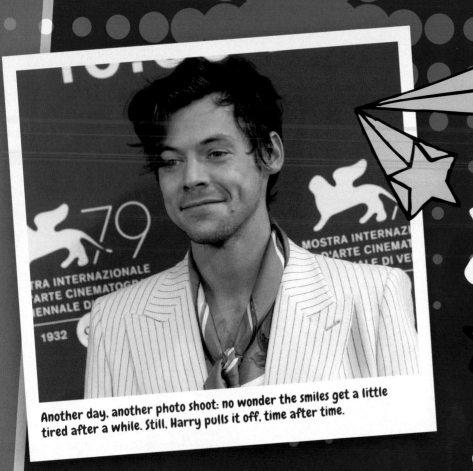

Another day, another photo shoot: no wonder the smiles get a little tired after a while. Still, Harry pulls it off, time after time.

did, for example. He made it through *The X Factor* through his own singing and dancing talent; his courage when it came to stepping out in front of 30,000 people; and because he smiled, remained friendly and gave it his best shot when he was asked to do difficult things. That's his first example to us all, right there.

Now, getting through *The X Factor* was the easy part, believe it or not. The real work came when One Direction suddenly became massive. Harry was then required to sing, dance and be entertaining for two hours a night on tour; be friendly and interesting in press and TV interviews all day; rehearse constantly; get on with four bandmates; stay fit; fly on endless, exhausting, long-haul

flights; sign autographs for the fans… and repeat that process for 100 to 200 days a year, for years on end.

I suggest that you or I would find that lifestyle fun for the first week, tops. After that, we'd start to slip: maybe a frustrated tantrum on a plane here, or a drunken crying session there. We'd be in the papers, we'd be told off by management, we might even be fired and sent home. Yes, we would.

Now, Harry never did any of that. He has always remained professional, he has always focused on the job in hand, he has never been seen falling out of nightclubs or overindulging in drink and drugs. The fact that he does all that is why he is a role model that we should all try to emulate.

Test your Harry knowledge!

CAN YOU HIT THE GOLDEN NOTE?

Q1: What are Harry's parents' names?

Q2: What three non-monetary assets does Harry have?

Q3: Who described Harry as a "good role model for everybody"?

Grab a notepad and pen and see how well you know Harry.
Answers on p122

Harry's fans are great, but can you imagine meeting thousands of them and having to smile and be chatty every single time?

"Harry was required to travel the world, sing like an angel and smile for the cameras after a 20-hour flight"

The rock star unleashed: Harry in 2018, finally able to explore music of his own choosing.

Evolution
of musical style

AND SO THE BOY BECOMES A MAN: THE STORY OF HARRY'S EVOLUTION AS A MUSICIAN

Sixteen years old is a young age to become a globally famous pop star. At that age, most of us can just about tie our shoelaces and get up for school on time, but in Harry's case, he was required to travel the world, sing like an angel and smile for the cameras after a 20-hour flight. It's no wonder that he didn't spend too much time thinking about music, but that was okay because One Direction had a team of songwriters doing that for them. And what was their job? To write pop music that kids aged two to 14 would like.

That explains the enjoyably sweet sounds of 1D's first album, *Up All Night* (2011), a bubblegum confection of catchy songs that sounded great when you sang them in the shower. Harry sang strongly for his age: check out 'Gotta Be You' for an example of his vocal range. When the next album, *Take Me Home*, came along in 2012, there was a slight movement towards more serious songs, 'slight' being the operative word; Harry showcased a softer side to his vocal style with 'Little Things' and 'They Don't Know About Us'.

k at their cheeky faces! One Direction in 2011, which feels like a lifetime ago.

It was 2013's *Midnight Memories* that revealed most growth in the 1D sound, enabling Harry to use a more adult voice on 'Little White Lies', 'You & I' and 'Story Of My Life'. The following year's *Four* and 2015's *Made In The A.M.* did more of the same, even though he focused more on ballad-indebted songs such as 'Clouds', 'Girl Almighty' and 'Spaces'.

Now, once Harry was free of the all-smiling, all-pop environment of One Direction, he was able to blossom into any musical territory he wanted – which explains why he went back to the classic Seventies music of his parents' record collections, and the guitar sounds he'd made at school with White Eskimo. On *Harry Styles* (2017), songs such as 'Woman' and 'Kiwi' had a clear rock feel, and he also delved into emotionally vulnerable territory with 'Two Ghosts' and 'Sweet Creature'. Meanwhile, 'Meet Me In The Hallway' had an indie sound, although the big hit, 'Sign Of The Times', was another heartfelt ballad.

By 2019's *Fine Line*, Harry had embraced a whole new musical aesthetic that included a wide range of influences. The title cut featured a trumpets-and-drums finale, while 'Lights Up' and 'Watermelon Sugar' focused on gospel pop and horns-driven funk respectively. As for 2022's masterpiece, *Harry's House*, the music may have a Japanese 'city pop' feel that is part-R&B and part-urban sounds, but it's difficult to sum it all up because there's just so much different stuff going on.

By this point, Harry has evolved from covering other artists' material, to singing songs written by professionals, to songs featuring his co-write credit, to his own material. A lot of musicians never get that far, especially as he's only 28 as we write this. That's the mark of a serious creative force, and we can't wait to see what he does next.

1D looked a bit different by 2015, didn't they? A million hours of plane travel will do that to you.

Tired of the music business, Harry changed jobs in 2021... just kidding! This is him acting in *My Policeman*.

Test your Harry knowledge!

CAN YOU HIT THE GOLDEN NOTE?

Q1: Name the years of release of 1D's five albums.

Q2: Which 1D album revealed the biggest growth in their sound?

Q3: Which two fruits are mentioned in this article?

Grab a notepad and pen and see how well you know Harry.
Answers on p122

Awards and accolades

STREWTH! HARRY'S GOING TO NEED A PRETTY LONG MANTELPIECE
IF HE WANTS TO DISPLAY THIS LOT ON IT...

Giz a smile, Harry! Accepting the award for Best Solo Performance at the 63rd Grammys in 2021.

Awards and accolades

Over the 12 years since Harry first became famous, he's been nominated for 130 awards, winning 46 of them. Mind you, we're writing this in late 2022: he'll probably win a load more by the time you read this...

The numbers speak for themselves. One Direction have sold more than 70 million albums to date, qualifying them as one of the best-selling boy bands of all time, and in a single year – 2013 – earned a massive $75 million, making them the second-highest earning celebrity (the five singers making up a single celeb, so to speak) under the age of 30. According to the Forbes organisation that makes this kind of list, 1D were the fourth-highest-earning celebrities in the world in 2015 and the second in 2016. Think about what that means for a moment.

As for physical trophies of the sort that you can take home and show your gran, 1D did well there too. Across their six-year career, the group nabbed seven Brit Awards, seven American Music Awards, six Billboard Music Awards, five Billboard Touring Awards and four MTV Video Music Awards. The Teen Choice panel particularly liked One Direction, nominating them for awards 31 times and actually giving them the honours on 28 occasions. (Who won the missing three awards, that's what we want to know?) In fact, they became the Teen Choice Awards' most awarded act.

"Is that a surfboard in your pocket etc?" It's the Teen Choice Awards 2013 in Universal City, California.

115

Test your Harry knowledge!

CAN YOU HIT THE GOLDEN NOTE?

🎵 **Q1:** How many albums have One Direction sold?

🎵 **Q2:** Which Harry single won an actual Grammy?

🎵 **Q3:** Which of his albums won Album of the Year at MTV's VMAs?

Grab a notepad and pen and see how well you know Harry.
Answers on p122

Rupert Everett, Harry, Emma Corrin, David Dawson, Gina McKee and Linus Roache with the TIFF Tribute Award for Performance for *My Policeman* in 2022.

Perhaps more seriously, the International Federation of the Phonographic Industry (IFPI) named One Direction the Global Recording Artist of the Year in 2013, while the following year Billboard made them Artist Of The Year. Who knows what else 1D would have won if they hadn't gone on a Ross-and-Rachel-style 'break' in 2016?

Once Harry's solo career kicked in, awards for him started flying in too. His song 'Sign Of The Times' won the Brit Award for British Video of the Year and the iHeartRadio Music Award for Best Music Video. His debut album bagged the ARIA Award for Best International Artist, the Australian equivalent of a Grammy, and two singles from his 2019 album *Fine Line* were recognised at the 2020 Global Awards and 2020 MTV Video Music Awards. *Fine Line* itself won the American Music Award for Favorite Pop/Rock Album and the Juno Award for

International Album of the Year, and was nominated for British Album of the Year at the 2020 Brit Awards.

The big news, awards-wise, was that Harry's single 'Watermelon Sugar' won an actual Grammy Award for Best Pop Solo Performance at the 63rd Annual Grammys in 2021. This is what all songwriters dream of, as it's the ultimate recognition from the music industry – the equivalent of an Oscar in the film world.

Don't forget that Harry has also been acclaimed as an actor: for the 2017 film *Dunkirk*, probably his best role to date, he got two acting ensemble nominations at the Critics' Choice Movie Awards and the Washington DC Area Film Critics Association Awards. His clothing choices have got him an industry nod here and there too, scooping a Fashion Award and no fewer than six Teen Choice Awards for his tasty wardrobe.

Future projects

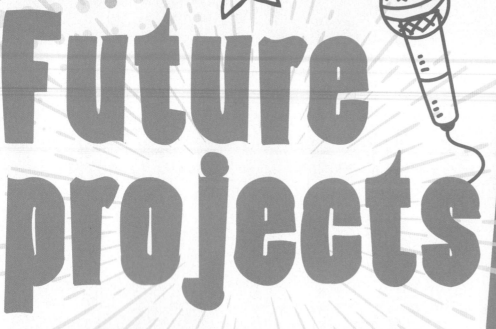

WHAT'S UP NEXT FOR HARRY, WORK-WISE? WE PEEK INTO HIS DIARY FOR 2023 AND BEYOND

What does a man plan to do with his life, when that man can do pretty much anything he wants?

Well, in the case of Harry Styles, several options are available to him as we write this – and many more will doubtless have opened up by the time you read these words. In order of how many people are spreading rumours and getting excited about a possible Styles career move, they go like this:

WILL HARRY APPEAR AS EROS IN THE NEXT *ETERNALS* MOVIE?

It seems that the answer may well be yes. After all, his little scene at the end of the first instalment was one of the best things about it – possibly the best for those who disliked the movie. Not only that, when Marvel Studios' president, Kevin Feige, was asked by *MTV News* about the return of the character at San Diego Comic-Con in July 2022, Feige said, "Yes, the adventures of Eros and [his sidekick] Pip is something that is very exciting for us." Now, this might just work, if Harry takes a few voice lessons anyway: his American accent was definitely a tad ropey in that cameo.

WILL HARRY APPEAR IN A NEW *STAR WARS* PRODUCTION?

This came from the website Giant Freakin Robot, which wrote in the summer of 2022 that according to 'trusted and proven sources', Harry 'is currently looking to join an upcoming *Star Wars* show'. A lot of fans got very excited about this idea – and why not? We can totally imagine him as a black-clad Darth Styles – but he poured cold water on the idea, telling *Rolling*

A question all Marvel and Harry Styles fans want to know – will he reprise his role as Eros? Guess we'll have to wait and see.

Our man in 2022, with multiple options ahead of him for '23 and beyond. Whatever he does next, it will be badass.

Stone: "That's the first I've heard of that. I'd imagine…false."

WILL HE BE IN A NEW BRAD PITT FILM CALLED FASTER, CHEAPER, BETTER?

A film distributor, Vértice Cine, posted on its website in August 2020 that Harry and Brad had been cast in this new movie from *Nightcrawler* director Dan Gilroy. Right after its announcement, sources told *Vanity Fair* that actually, neither bloke had been confirmed to feature in the film. So, probably not then.

Will he be doing any acting at all? Perhaps. As he told *Rolling Stone*: "I think there'll be a time again when I'll crave it. But when you're making music, something's happening. It feels really creative, and it feeds stuff. A large part of acting is the doing-nothing, waiting thing. Which if that's the worst part, then it's a pretty good job. But I don't find that section of it to be that fulfilling. I like doing it in the moment, but I don't think I'll do it a lot."

WILL HE BE MAKING NEW MUSIC?

Nothing has been announced, but the country singer Shania Twain – who performed live with Harry at 2022's Coachella Festival – wants to do a collaboration of some sort with him. "In the future, I would say yeah," she told Extra. "I'm going to hold him to that… I think we surprised each other… just how natural it was."

IS HE GOING TO KEEP BUILDING THE STYLES PRODUCTS EMPIRE?

We assume so. After all, he has a skin care, nail polish and clothing line called Pleasing, and a fashion collection with Gucci.

IS HE GOING TO BE A DAD?

Not that we've heard, but he did recently say, "If I have kids at some point, I will encourage them to be themselves and be vulnerable and share," so he's clearly given the matter some thought.

IS HE GOING TO TAKE TIME OFF?

Perhaps, to work on his imperfections, as he mused: "The fantasy, or the vision, or the version of you that people can build you up to be feels like a person that isn't flawed," he said. "What I value the most from my friends is I feel like I'm constantly reminded that it's okay to be flawed. I think I'm pretty messy and make mistakes sometimes. I think that's the most loving thing: you can see someone's imperfections, and it's not [that you] love them in spite of that, but it's [that you] love them with that."

If that's the lesson you take away from this publication, readers, then Harry will no doubt be a happy man.

That does impress her much: Shania Twain sings at Coachella with Harry.

We're hopeful there'll be plenty more arena shows, festivals and world tours to look forward to in the near future.

Test your Harry knowledge!

CAN YOU HIT THE GOLDEN NOTE?

🎵 **Q1:** Who is Eros's sidekick?

🎵 **Q2:** Who played with Harry at Coachella?

🎵 **Q3:** What is Harry's final message?

Grab a notepad and pen and see how well you know Harry.
Answers on p122

The answers

SO, HOW WELL DO YOU KNOW HARRY STYLES? FIND OUT HERE!

Early life

Answer 1 - **BRONZE** (1 point)

Redditch, Worcestershire

Answer 2 - **SILVER** (2 points)

Gemma

Answer 3 - **GOLD** (3 points)

'The Girl of My Best Friend'

School days

Answer 1 - **BRONZE** (1 point)

Hermitage School

Answer 2 - **SILVER** (2 points)

Mrs Vernon

Answer 3 - **GOLD** (3 points)

"I'm going, oh, I'm going home."

Taking Pride: Harry Styles in New York at the Music Hall of Williamsburg in 2020.

122

0-39 points **You need some serious 1D and HS education!**
40-79 points **You've put in some study time, but must try harder.**
80-119 points **Not bad at all. Harry would be proud of you.**
120-149 points **Your HS expertise makes you a Styles superfan.**
150-174 points **You are Harry Styles. Cheat!**

First band

Answer 1 - **BRONZE** (1 point)
Cheese And Crackers

Answer 2 - **SILVER** (2 points)
Jet

Answer 3 - **GOLD** (3 points)
Yes, they are!

X Factor: Solo

Answer 1 - **BRONZE** (1 point)
A scarf and cardigan

Answer 2 - **SILVER** (2 points)
Gemma Styles

Answer 3 - **GOLD** (3 points)
Louis Walsh

X Factor: One Direction

Answer 1 - **BRONZE** (1 point)
Niall Horan, Liam Payne, Louis Tomlinson and Zayn Malik

Answer 2 - **SILVER** (2 points)
Matt Cardle and Rebecca Ferguson

Answer 3 - **GOLD** (3 points)
Simon Cowell

The birth of 1D

Answer 1 - **BRONZE** (1 point)
Harry Potter And The Deathly Hallows: Part 1

Answer 2 - **SILVER** (2 points)
Louis Tomlinson

Answer 3 - **GOLD** (3 points)
Rihanna's 'Only Girl (In The World)', 'Chasing Cars' by Snow Patrol, 'Kids In America' by Kim Wilde, Kelly Clarkson's 'My Life Would Suck Without You' and 'Forever Young'.

Up All Night

Answer 1 - **BRONZE** (1 point)
Savan Kotecha

Answer 2 - **SILVER** (2 points)
Radio City

Answer 3 - **GOLD** (3 points)
4.5 million

And they're off! Harry and Olivia head off into the sunset. Missing you already, guys...

Rocking a pearl necklace as only a modern pop star can.

Take Me Home

Answer 1 - BRONZE (1 point)
Virginia Woolf

Answer 2 - SILVER (2 points)
Emma Ostilly

Answer 3 - GOLD (3 points)
London

Midnight Memories

Answer 1 - BRONZE (1 point)
Julian Bunetta and John Ryan

Answer 2 - SILVER (2 points)
Taylor Swift

Answer 3 - GOLD (3 points)
Four million

Four

Answer 1 - BRONZE (1 point)
Paul Dugdale

Answer 2 - SILVER (2 points)
$15 million

Answer 3 - GOLD (3 points)
200th

Made In The A.M.

Answer 1 - BRONZE (1 point)
25 March 2015

Answer 2 - SILVER (2 points)
Sophie Muller

Answer 3 - GOLD (3 points)
'History'

The end of 1D

Answer 1 - **BRONZE** (1 point)

Zayn wanted to relax and enjoy time in private

Answer 2 - **SILVER** (2 points)

August 2015

Answer 3 - **GOLD** (3 points)

Sheffield, UK

Going solo

Answer 1 - **BRONZE** (1 point)

Erskine Records

Answer 2 - **SILVER** (2 points)

Jamaica (or the Caribbean)

Answer 3 - **GOLD** (3 points)

May 2017

Harry Styles: The album

Answer 1 - **BRONZE** (1 point)

Nick Grimshaw

Answer 2 - **SILVER** (2 points)

'Sign Of The Times'

Answer 3 - **GOLD** (3 points)

San Francisco

Dunkirk

Answer 1 - **BRONZE** (1 point)

Alex

Answer 2 - **SILVER** (2 points)

$522 million

Answer 3 - **GOLD** (3 points)

Around $3.4 million

There's plenty for Harry to celebrate at the moment, with more good times ahead we imagine.

Harry's fans

Answer 1 - **BRONZE** (1 point)

London Road

Answer 2 - **SILVER** (2 points)

Twemlow railway viaduct

Answer 3 - **GOLD** (3 points)

Stylers (or Harries)

Fashion

Answer 1 - **BRONZE** (1 point)

BS

Answer 2 - **SILVER** (2 points)

Harry Lambert

Answer 3 - **GOLD** (3 points)

True (in 2020)

Fine Line

Answer 1 - **BRONZE** (1 point)

Camille Rowe

Answer 2 - **SILVER** (2 points)

Treat People With Kindness

Answer 3 - **GOLD** (3 points)

Actress Phoebe Waller-Bridge

On tour

Answer 1 - **BRONZE** (1 point)

Niall Horan

Answer 2 - **SILVER** (2 points)

£100 million

Answer 3 - **GOLD** (3 points)

89

Small screen

Answer 1 - **BRONZE** (1 point)

Madison McMillin

Answer 2 - **SILVER** (2 points)

Mick Jagger

Answer 3 - **GOLD** (3 points)

Saturday Night Live

A kiss goodbye: Harry says farewell for now, but he'll be back.

Philanthropy and advocacy

Answer 1 - **BRONZE** (1 point)

£100 million

Answer 2 - **SILVER** (2 points)

Ghana

Answer 3 - **GOLD** (3 points)

True

Treat People With Kindness

Answer 1 - **BRONZE** (1 point)

Do You Know Who You Are

Answer 2 - **SILVER** (2 points)

Grace

Answer 3 - **GOLD** (3 points)

Fine Line

Personal life

Answer 1 - **BRONZE** (1 point)

£100 million

Answer 2 - **SILVER** (2 points)

Tequila and wine

Answer 3 - **GOLD** (3 points)

Film director

Harry's House

Answer 1 - **BRONZE** (1 point)

Haruomi Hosono

Answer 2 - **SILVER** (2 points)

'As It Was', 'Late Night Talking', 'Music For A Sushi Restaurant'

Answer 3 - **GOLD** (3 points)

15 weeks

Silver screen

Answer 1 - **BRONZE** (1 point)

Eros

Answer 2 - **SILVER** (2 points)

Brighton

Answer 3 - **GOLD** (3 points)

Elvis

Role model

Answer 1 - **BRONZE** (1 point)

Anne and Des

Answer 2 - **SILVER** (2 points)

A loving family, a decent education and a trauma-free upbringing

Answer 3 - **GOLD** (3 points)

The Darkness's Justin Hawkins

Evolution of musical style

Answer 1 - **BRONZE** (1 point)

2011, 2012, 2013, 2014, 2015

Answer 2 - **SILVER** (2 points)

Midnight Memories

Answer 3 - **GOLD** (3 points)

Kiwi and watermelon

Awards and accolades

Answer 1 - **BRONZE** (1 point)

More than 70 million

Answer 2 - **SILVER** (2 points)

'Watermelon Sugar'

Answer 3 - **GOLD** (3 points)

Harry's House in 2022

Future projects

Answer 1 - **BRONZE** (1 point)

Pip

Answer 2 - **SILVER** (2 points)

Shania Twain

Answer 3 - **GOLD** (3 points)

It's okay to be flawed!

All answers correct as of 16 November 2022

Images: Getty Images

Celebrate the songs and sounds of the greatest decades in music

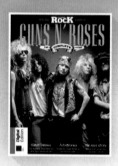

Explore the lives and legacies of some of the world's most iconic artists

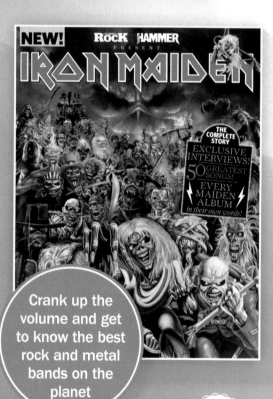

Crank up the volume and get to know the best rock and metal bands on the planet

Get great savings when you buy direct from us

1000s of great titles, many not available anywhere else

World-wide delivery and super-safe ordering

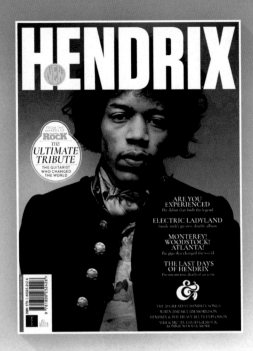

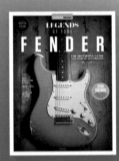

HOW WELL DO YOU KNOW
HARRY?

Future PLC Quay House, The Ambury, Bath, BA1 1UA

Editorial
Author **Joel McIver**
Editor **Dan Peel**
Senior Designer **Adam Markiewicz**
Senior Art Editor **Andy Downes**
Head of Art & Design **Greg Whitaker**
Editorial Director **Jon White**

Cover images
Getty Images

Photography
All copyrights and trademarks are recognised and respected

Advertising
Media packs are available on request
Commercial Director **Clare Dove**

International
Head of Print Licensing **Rachel Shaw**
licensing@futurenet.com
www.futurecontenthub.com

Circulation
Head of Newstrade **Tim Mathers**

Production
Head of Production **Mark Constance**
Production Project Manager **Matthew Eglinton**
Advertising Production Manager **Joanne Crosby**
Digital Editions Controller **Jason Hudson**
Production Managers **Keely Miller, Nola Cokely,
Vivienne Calvert, Fran Twentyman**

Printed in the UK

Distributed by Marketforce, 5 Churchill Place, Canary Wharf, London, E14 5HU
www.marketforce.co.uk Tel: 0203 787 9001

How Well Do You Know Harry? First Edition (MUB4795)
© 2022 Future Publishing Limited

FUTURE

Connectors.
Creators.
Experience
Makers.

Future plc is a public
company quoted on the
London Stock Exchange
(symbol: FUTR)
www.futureplc.com

Chief executive **Zillah Byng-Thorne**
Non-executive chairman **Richard Huntingford**
Chief financial officer **Penny Ladkin-Brand**

Tel +44 (0)1225 442 244

Widely
Recycled

ipso.
For press freedom
with responsibility